MOMENTS

THE
PULITZER PRIZE
PHOTOGRAPHS

UPDATED EDITION: 1942-1982

MOMENTS

THE PULITZER PRIZE PHOTOGRAPHS

UPDATED EDITION: 1942-1982

Sheryle and John Leekley

CROWN PUBLISHERS, INC., NEW YORK

Inquiries should be addressed to Crown Publishers, Inc., One Park Avenue,
New York, N.Y. 10016

Printed in the United States of America
Published simultaneously in Canada by General Publishing Company Limited

LOU REDA PRODUCTIONS

Book Design: Huguette Franco

Library of Congress Cataloging in Publication Data

Leekley, Sheryle.
   Moments: the Pulitzer Prize photographs. Updated
   edition: 1942–1982

   1. Photography, Journalistic—Awards.   2. Pulitzer
prizes.   I. Leekley, John.   II. Title.
TR820.L43   1982   779′.0973   82-18252
ISBN 0-517-54736-8

10 9 8 7 6 5 4 3 2 1
First Updated Edition

Contents

The camera seems to me, next to unassisted
and weaponless consciousness, the central
instrument of our time.

James Agee

Let Us Now Praise Famous Men

Introduction

The Pulitzer Prize represents the pinnacle of achievement in the field of American journalism. It is an annual award, endowed by newspaper publisher Joseph Pulitzer (1847–1911), in a bequest to Columbia University in New York City. There are twelve categories for journalism, of which two are photography—spot-news and feature. A panel of eminent editors and journalists from around the country serves as nominating jurors, recommending three choices in both categories of photography from among all the entries. The Pulitzer Prize Board then selects that year's winners, taking into consideration the choices of the nominating jurors but not necessarily bound to them. These decisions are announced by the president of Columbia University in April of each year.

The first award for photography was presented in 1942 and, except for 1946, has been given in each succeeding year. In 1968, the photography category was expanded to include feature photography, where photos are not primarily dependent on the time value of a news event, as they are in spot news. Instead, the value is in its penetrating coverage of important issues and subjects.

The feature category, and increasingly since 1979 the spot-news category, is often composed of a series of pictures that tends to provide a more filmic, documentary approach. This contrasts with the earlier awards, almost all single photographs, which tended toward an elliptical shorthand in telling a story, where images function as symbols or moral statements.

The Pulitzer Prize collection has great personal significance. The lasting impression in the minds of most Americans about many major events is often made by that year's Pulitzer Prize photograph. In fact, we mark our lifetimes by remembering what we were doing when we first saw those images: the girl crying out in anguish at Kent State . . . the children napalmed in Vietnam, running and screaming down the road . . . the shooting of Lee Harvey Oswald . . . the hole in Adlai Stevenson's shoe . . . Marines raising the flag at Iwo Jima. These frozen moments have been etched into the minds and hearts of everyone.

These photographs are authentic Americana, signposts along the way in the history of our nation. Yet, they have been largely overlooked as documents of our past and testimony to our present.

For the first time, this book brings together the Pulitzer Prize photographs from each year into one volume, and tells the story behind each one. Each moment is the intersection of lifelines—the photographer's and those of the people whose lives or deaths are recorded. And the whole is surely greater than the sum of its parts. The total impact of this collection evokes an emotional response that could not have been predicted.

In the preparation of this book, we have interviewed the Pulitzer Prize winners in photography from 1942 to 1982. We worked closely with them in all details. We also spoke with the families and friends of those photographers who are deceased.

In all cases, the print we used was of the highest possible quality. Many times, the photographers themselves made a print for us from the original negatives. If the award was for a series of photographs, and we could not reproduce all of them (some numbered as many as sixty), the photographer chose those that would best represent his work.

As we got to know the photographers better, our respect for them developed into a kind of awe . . . for their personal courage, dedication, and "heart." It was this passion that enabled them to capture the sense of their times in one fleeting moment.

Perhaps more than any other single factor, we see a great deal of violence in these photographs, reflecting the violence in life around us. But, just as our lives consist of other factors, here, too, we find bravery, compassion, dedication, joy, and so much more of the day-to-day human qualities that surround us. These photographs record the drama of life and death . . . and everything between. They are moments of history.

Foreword
Dan Rather

There is such a haunting quality to Pulitzer Prize photographs, whatever the year and regardless of how many times you look at them.

There we are, the way we were.

The world turns, the clock moves but there we are again.

It has been five years since I wrote the foreword to the first edition of *Moments: The Pulitzer Prize Photographs.* That haunting quality persists and, if anything, grows stronger with the addition of the latest award winners in this new, updated edition.

Take a look at Skeeter Hagler's 1980 collection of cowboys. Gaze and wonder at these remembrances of things past and reminders of things present. Take a look at Nick Ut's 1972 photograph of the little Vietnamese girl bathed in napalm. I don't know that any of us who covered the war in Vietnam summed up the experience as memorably as the man who said "War is Hell" more than a century ago, but even that celebrated truism doesn't paint the green-jungle hell that was Vietnam as graphically as Ut's photograph. Hell is a private vision.

And so it is with other photographs, old and new, in this book: Winners in Iran execute losers (1980, Anonymous, UPI); the hunters and the hunted in Pottstown, Pa. (1979, Tom Kelly, *The Mercury*); South Vietnam's national police chief executes a Vietcong commando (1969, Eddie Adams, AP); refugees flee over the bombed-out bridge at Pyongyang (1951, Max Desfor, AP). These are universal messages. They invite us to share hell.

"We see a great deal of violence in these photographs," the Leekleys write. ". . . perhaps reflecting the violence in life around us." Not all of it in war, they might add. Consider Don Ultang's and John Robinson's *Des Moines Register* sequence, showing a black football star leveled for daring to play against a team of white men. Look, and remember that the year was 1951—in the United States of America. If you'll forgive the metaphor, we Americans have gained some yardage since.

But there's no need to be portentous. Life isn't, and this book of photographs reflecting on life isn't either. I don't care how you vote, the famous photograph of Adlai Stevenson "baring his sole" will touch you. Few people who saw it forgot that picture, but I'll bet you that not one in a hundred—and I include myself in the majority—would remember the photographer as Bill Gallagher of the *Flint Journal.* Redressing that ignorance is just another attribute of this valuable book.

Among its other virtues, the volume you hold in your hands is a fitting companion for Gerald W. Johnson's *The Lines Are Drawn,* a 1958 collection of Pulitzer Prize-winning cartoons. Johnson argued that, for various reasons, the Pulitzer cartoonists frequently were honored for work that didn't measure up to their best. I don't speak from certainty, but I doubt that you could make the same criticism about this collection.

But it's time to raise the curtain—or should I say, "open the shutter"? On another occasion, I wrote, "The camera never blinks." In some ways, that is truer of still photographs than of televised pictures. They do not flicker or blur, they are not interrupted by a commercial, they are not evanescent.

Study them if you would know a little more about history, about your times—and perhaps about yourself.

Acknowledgment

We would like to thank the photographers and their families, who shared with us their lives and experiences. And thanks to all the people at Columbia University who gave us so much support and cooperation, especially Dr. Richard Baker, Rose Valenstein, Fred Knubel, Nancy Carmody, Mary Murphy, and Jonathan Beard. Also, a special thanks to Lou Reda, Herb Michelman, Jerry Cammarata, and Howard Price.

MOMENTS
THE
PULITZER PRIZE
PHOTOGRAPHS
UPDATED EDITION: 1942-1982

1942 Battle on the Picket Lines

Stones, fists, and steel bars. Unionism grows up with violence, fighting for its birthright on the streets. While the world is at war in Europe, the streets of America rage in heated controversy over the legality of this radical young power.

On May 26, 1937, United Auto Workers officers and organizers attempt to leaflet at the plant gates of Ford Motor Company. Ford Company men come down on them, causing an all-out riot and scores of injuries. The Ford Company is found guilty of unfair labor practices under the Wagner Act and ordered to open its doors to unionization. Four years later, the union organizers, the courts, and the National Labor Relations Board are still slugging it out with big Henry Ford.

Now the front lines of this battle are being drawn on the grounds of the River Rouge plant of Ford Motor Company— Ford's Goliath. April 2 . . . a Union committeeman in the rolling mill is fired. Soon after, 6,000 employees in the rolling mill stop work, followed by the open-hearth and pressed-steel plants— another 15,000 employees. The word is out . . . strike!

Department after department shuts down. A Ford railroad engine passes the gates with its whistle tied down as strikers at the gates cheer and sing. Squads of unionists roam the length of the plant, shouting "Come on out" to nonstrikers. Charging out of the plant, groups of strikebreakers and Ford goons descend on them. Emotions boil on the picket lines as iron bolts, hammers, and wrenches fill the air on this April morning in 1941.

Never before in the thirty-eight-year history of Ford Motor Company has a strike closed any of the Ford plants in Detroit. By closing ranks, the auto workers stand up to marauding strikebreakers and state police. The fight for a united labor movement grows upon these bold and pioneering foundations. Although the strikers lose this battle, history will show that they win the war.

Milton (Pete) Brooks of the *Detroit News* waits patiently for a good shot. He watches the drama unfold and, when the confrontation explodes into violence, he moves in to record the moment . . . capturing in a startling way the fury and the power that gives the unions life.

And Brooks comes away with more than a good shot. It is the first in a tradition of great news photographs to be awarded the Pulitzer Prize.

1943 The Castaways

Frank "Pappy" Noel, veteran AP photographer, is walking in downtown Singapore. He's unsteady on his feet, and stops to rest against a building. He is sweaty and feverish, shivering with malaria. Then the bombs fall . . . the siege of Singapore has begun.

It has only been a few weeks since the Japanese surprised Pearl Harbor, and they have already driven the Allied forces across the Malayan jungle in a disastrous retreat. Pappy was there with the Allies through the worst of it. As he runs for cover, he knows Singapore will soon fall. He's got to get out.

He pays his way onto a British freighter heading for Rangoon. It's midnight, 270 miles off Sumatra . . . they feel safe now.

As Pappy sleeps fitfully in his cabin, a Japanese torpedo crashes into the ship, blowing a gaping hole in her side. She begins to sink. Pappy tries to get out, but his door is jammed shut. In desperation, he smashes through it. Out of seventy-seven crewmen, twenty-seven get to the lifeboats. This is the first warning the Allies have that Japanese submarines are prowling the Indian Ocean.

For days the lifeboats bob hopelessly in the ocean. On the third day, another lifeboat drifts by Noel's. An Indian sailor begs for water. Their water casks were smashed during the launching from the stricken ship . . . they will die without water. Noel shakes his head helplessly. There is no water.

Pappy does the only thing he can do; he lifts his camera and records this moment of contact in the middle of the ocean. Almost immediately, a monsoon is upon them, and the lifeboats are scattered. Pappy is rescued two days later, nearly dead. The Indian's boat and another are lost at sea.

1944 The Willingness to Die

The hell that is Tarawa. In the 168-year history of the United States Marine Corps, there is no victory quite as bittersweet as the taking of Tarawa. Out of the 3,000 American assault forces, only a few hundred escape death or wounds.

Tarawa is untouchable, the Japanese boast. Four thousand Japanese soldiers are sheltered underground in concrete blockhouses with walls five feet thick, reinforced by palm trees eighteen inches wide and steel rails. And, on top of it all, a ten-foot blanket of sand and coral. The military brass agree that nothing but a direct hit or a 2,000-pound bomb could destroy these blockhouses. The steely Japanese must be rooted out of the earth itself.

The three-day battle begins. Preparatory shelling and bombing leave the island a litter of splintered coconut palms and shattered concrete. After this softening up, the marines mount their amphibious assault.

They come in waves from the landing boats, one group at a time, pushing through over-the-head water onto the shallows and the beachhead. Facing them is a solid wall of enemy gunfire coming from inside the concrete pillboxes. They are walking into a bloodbath—certain death for many of the seasoned leathernecks. They keep coming, firing and dying, until at last they charge over the bodies of the fallen and wipe out the Japanese gunners.

Frank Filan, combat photographer for Associated Press, is on one of the advance landing boats off Tarawa. His boat is hit and sinking fast. Weighted down with camera equipment, he swims madly to shore through the intense spray of gunfire. He stops to help a wounded comrade who is trying to return to a landing boat several hundred yards behind. After swimming fifty yards under heavy fire, Filan realizes they will never make the boat. He persuades the injured marine that they should push for the beach again. Sinking deep into bomb craters as they go, they finally reach the shore. But the cameras are ruined.

"The first two days I spent on Tarawa were the worst of my life. There I was, with a war going on all around my ears, and not a thing to take a picture with." On the third day, Filan borrows a camera from a coast guard photographer and pushes ahead with the diehard veterans to record this desperate struggle.

In seventy-six hours, the Japanese garrison of 4,000 is destroyed, almost to the last man. Many are buried alive beneath the rubble. Flame throwers leave hundreds of charred, bloated bodies as testimony on the Tarawa sands.

Not since Pickett's charge of the Civil War have American recruits been so willing to make the ultimate sacrifice. It is this unflinching heroism and willingness to die that wins the battle against a determined foe . . . who submits only in total annihilation.

1944 Home Is the Hero

War scenes have been a fact of life these last few years. The war touches every American family—victory gardens, gas coupons, meat and sugar rations. Prewar housewives turn Rosie the Riveter to keep the factories running. Hundreds of thousands of men go off to war, and day by day the wounded heroes return.

Lieutenant Colonel Robert Moore is coming home. Home is Villisca, Iowa, population 1,100. The whole town awaits its returning son at the train station. A veteran of the North African Campaign against Rommel's rugged Panzer Corps and hero of Faïd Pass, he is a recipient of the Distinguished Service Cross. He leaves behind places like Casablanca, Tobruk, and Tripoli for heartland America. A crowd of well-wishers gathers in jubilant anticipation.

Earl Bunker of the *Omaha World-Herald* waits for almost a full twenty-four hours to capture this timeless moment . . . the returning soldier. On the morning of July 15, 1943, Moore's train pulls into Villisca. From out of the crowds on the waiting platform, Dorothy and Nancy Moore rush forward. Bunker catches the spontaneous joy of a reunited family as Moore crushes seven-year-old Nancy in his arms. We see the other side of war, people who go on through it all . . . still living and loving.

1945 Iwo Jima

Iwo is an unlikely jewel. Just a miserable plot of volcanic ash, it is one of a series of small islands about 650 miles south of Tokyo. But a prize jewel nonetheless, for its capture promises further security in the Pacific and a strategically close strike-posture against Japan.

It is 1945. America has been hard at war for four years. Much of the territory taken by the Japanese in those terrible early years has been reclaimed, causing a shift in the balance of power. The Pacific is on its way to becoming a "U.S. ocean." But a final, sweeping campaign is needed to overwhelm the Japanese morale as well as its territory—a simultaneous raid on Tokyo Bay and Iwo Jima to split the already weak Japanese forces. For war-weary America, the time has come to sew up the Pacific.

At Iwo Jima, an all-out effort is launched. Seventy-two days of continual shelling and bombing, from the air and from the sea, obliterates the face of the island. But it fails to rout the 23,000 grizzled Japanese veterans secured in caves and concrete strongholds underground. This dirty job goes to the marines.

February 19 . . . the Fourth and Fifth Marines land on Iwo, headed for Mount Suribachi. It takes three days before they fight their way to the base of the mountain and four days till they surround it. The battle of Iwo Jima unfolds as one of the bloodiest encounters of the Pacific; the road to Suribachi is littered with the bodies of 6,821 men cut down and 19,217 maimed. On the morning of February 23, Company E, Second Battalion of the Twenty-eighth Regiment, makes the treacherous 550-foot climb up the rough and crusty mountainside. With what little energy they have left, they hoist the Stars and Stripes.

Joe Rosenthal, photographer, arrives on Iwo after campaigns on Guam, Peleliu, and Anguar. He gets word from a boatswain that a patrol is going up the mountain with a flag. Rosenthal and other photographers head toward Suribachi, picking their way through the land mines. When they reach the command post of the Twenty-eighth Regiment, they are told that a forty-man detachment has already started off with a flag.

On the way up the hill, they run for cover six times as the marines continue to blast Japanese snipers out of the caves.

Magazine photographers on their way down tell Rosenthal's group that the flag has already been raised. Joe is determined to get a shot anyway. Just before noon, they reach the top.

In the distance, Rosenthal sees a group of marines carrying a twenty-foot iron pipe and a huge American flag. He backs away about thirty-five feet and quickly piles up some stones and a sandbag to give him an added two feet. Out of the corner of his eye, he sees the six men straining against the big flag. Joe climbs on his pile and snaps the most famous of all war photographs. "In a way, it is a picture of a miracle. No man who survived that beach can tell you how he did it. It was like walking through rain and not getting wet. . . ."

Six men are frozen forever in the history of the nation—Ira Hayes, Franklyn Sousley, Harlan Block, Michael Strank, John Bradley, and Rene Gagnon. For that single image spoke for all America . . . about her pride, her valor, her sacrifice.

1947 A Face in Every Window

When W. F. Winecoff built his huge hotel in 1913, he took advantage of a quirk in the Atlanta building code. No fire escape was required by law if the building sat on a lot of less than 5,000 square feet. The Winecoff sat on 4,386. For thirty-three years, the full significance of this fact lay dormant . . . a sleeping holocaust.

Now, in the chilly predawn hours of December 7, 1946, the inevitable happens . . . fire! Sometime after 3:00 A.M. it starts. Where and how is still a question. Creeping down the hallway, the flames find the stairwell that runs up the center of the building like a chimney. The draft of air traveling up the stairwell fans the flames, till they roar through the hotel, floor by floor, seeking out the 285 people asleep in their beds.

At about 3:40, the bellboy discovers the fire and spreads the alarm. People come out of their rooms to get to the stairs . . . but it's a trap. The stairs have no fire doors. Many are caught by the smoke and gases before they can find their rooms again.

For those who make it back to their rooms, there is only one way out . . . the windows. The fire trucks arrive, extending their ladders as far as they can go—nine floors. The Winecoff Hotel is fifteen floors high. Those above are trapped.

They peer down, a face in every window. The firemen are helpless to save them.

On the back side of the hotel, a ten-foot alley separates the Winecoff and the Mortgage Guarantee Building. People try leaping across the gulf. They start falling, hitting with a sickening crunch. The alley begins to fill with bodies, the carnage too much for the firemen to bear.

Arnold Hardy, a student at Georgia Tech and amateur photographer, hears the general alarm. He runs three blocks to find a cab and arrives at 4:14.

"People were already falling to the sidewalks, trying to get out. They were rigging up bedsheet ladders, which would tear, or trying to climb from one window to another and falling. I was completely appalled that in modern times a thing like this could happen . . . that there was no way of preventing it, not some way of reaching these people. The firemen were working frantically trying to get them out, but the ladders wouldn't reach high enough. I could see only two life nets and one of those tore. I counted fourteen pieces of fire equipment and only one net being used.

"I saw eight or ten people fall. The woman I photographed was climbing down a rope that was hanging from a fire ladder. She had come out of a window below the top of the ladder. She could not reach the ladder, but she did get the rope. She got halfway down, and just hung there. She didn't have the strength to hold on. . . . She just dropped. I raised my camera, sighted her falling and clicked the shutter.

"She lived. It was a miracle. Her fall was arrested by a pipe that held up the marquee at the Peachtree entrance. She hit that, then she hit an iron railing around the marquee, and then she fell to the street. All of these were terrific impacts but . . . they saved her life.

"One woman threw her two children out. The firemen anticipated what she was going to do and shouted, 'Wait, don't throw them!' They were trying to get a net crew into position. But she didn't hear them. She threw them, and they were killed instantly. We saw her just collapse back into the flame-filled room to die.

"I saw this teenaged girl climb out from a window on the eighth or ninth floor and, somehow, digging her fingers and her toes into the cracks between the bricks, edge over toward another window. We all watched in horror for maybe fifteen minutes. She was like a spider against the wall. Later when I looked up again to see if she was still there, she was gone."

Sunrise. It is quiet. The crowd out front stands in sorrow. Inside, the firemen silently go about the ghastly business of finding the bodies. They don't talk much to each other; they just move from door to door, among the black shapes. On the fourteenth floor, they find W. F. Winecoff and his wife in their apartment, still in bed. They are both dead.

There is some joy: Those people on the top floors who had sealed their doors off from the smoke and gases and laid down on the floors of their rooms had lived.

One hundred and nineteen people died in the Winecoff fire. It was the worst hotel fire in history.

The Winecoff still stands today, looking much like it did then. Only now there are fire escapes. But, in the chilly predawn, you can almost see faces in the windows.

1948 Boy Gunman

As Patrolmen Jim Bray and Charley McCloskey cruise through Boston's Washington Park, they spot a kid rolling up a bolt of cloth. His name is Ed Bancroft; he is only fifteen years old . . . but he's a tough customer. When they stop to question him, he pulls a .32 from his pocket and opens fire, blasting holes in the police car and wounding Bray in the arm.

They chase him down to Paulding Street, near the Lewis School, where he grabs another fifteen-year-old boy, Bill Rowan. Using Rowan as a shield, he ducks into an alley at Dale and Walnut streets.

Photographer Frank Cushing sits a few blocks away, in the *Boston Herald* radio car, outside the Roxbury Howard Johnson's. There has just been a stickup in the restaurant, and he's waiting to photograph the victims. It's a warm New England summer day. Frank is in no hurry. A police car is parked next to him, the radio crackling with activity. Suddenly, the news comes across about a gun battle down the street. Cushing speeds away, pulling out his camera as he goes.

By the time Cushing arrives at the scene, the boy gunman has made his stand in the alley, daring the cops to come and get him, firing at the police. Crouching low, Cushing moves quickly down to the end of the alley. He takes a long shot down the length of the alley by holding the camera above his head, to keep from being shot. But he's not satisfied. He's too far from the action.

He runs around to a house backing on the alley and talks the woman in the house into letting him go upstairs. He climbs out on the roof and takes the picture. "I was wondering if the kid would shoot me. But I wanted that picture."

By now, there are police from three divisions bottling up the alley—twenty-seven cops and two fifteen-year-old boys. The police are taking positions in buildings and on rooftops surrounding the alley. As they close in, Bancroft yells out, "Don't come closer or I'll kill him," and he fires again at the police.

Officer Joe Toland is quietly crawling along the fence behind the two boys. Just as Bancroft sticks the .32 into Rowan's back, Toland stands up and slugs him with the butt of his gun. The drama ends as suddenly as it began.

Both boys are lucky to be alive.

24

1949 The King of Clout, the Sultan of Swat

The Babe . . . the unforgettable giant of baseball. From the time he hit the majors in 1914 until his death in 1948, he headlined his way through life, as much for his splashy style as for his string of record-breakers. The King of Clout, Sultan of Swat, he always gave the fans something to bring home with them. And they have never forgotten him for that. They are here, today, fifteen years after his last season, to give him something in return for all the magic memories and good times he brought to them. It is George Herman Ruth's formal farewell to baseball.

June 1948. It has been twenty-one years now since the likes of Lou Gehrig and the fabulous 1927 Yankees. Today, stoop-shouldered and unsteady, the demigod stands alone on the playing field of Yankee Stadium, surrounded by thousands of cheering fans.

And as he stands, older and more mellowed, they remember. They remember the bawdy, big-hearted oaf who hit baseball with a strong shot of pizazz. They remember the happy-go-lucky carouser, the gambler, the limelight-loving celebrity. They remember the athlete who had his own style of "training"—smoking twenty cigars a day, downing six and eight train-station franks as between-meal snacks, and washing them down with cans of beer and soda pop. They remember the devoted ambassador to the nation's hospitals, orphanages, and prisons, and the sentimental softy who could be persuaded to reform his rowdy ways on behalf of the "dirty-faced kids on the streets." Babe roared along with the twenties!

No one packs the stands like the Babe. They jam Yankee Stadium to watch that big bear with the massive torso and the bandy legs wrap his bat around the ball. "Slambino," the powerhouse slugger, leaves behind batting records that stand untouched for years.

Fact is—it doesn't matter much whether he pounds one home, strikes out, or just faces down the pitcher. In every case, the showmanship is unbeatable. He drives the fans so crazy with excitement that they are ready to tear up the stands. A base on balls is enough to cause pandemonium. And nobody can strike out with as much gusto.

This is a man who boldly plays to the crowds and then delivers. In his last World Series—Chicago, 1932—he is up at bat. The hostile Chicago fans are riding him, out of fear. He has

already popped one out of the park. He has two strikes on him now. He swats the air with a few practice swings. Before the next pitch is fired, he turns to the crowd, pointing to the flagpole. The pitch is delivered, and Babe sends it flying high above the flagpole.

Nat Fein, *New York Herald-Tribune* photographer, stands behind Babe. "The Number 3 was the thing I was interested in. I felt the only way to tell the story of Babe retiring was from the back. They retired his uniform that day, so that no other player would ever wear it again."

Eyes are misty and throats thick as fans get a last chance to cheer him on. In two months, he will pass away, but the legend lives still.

1950 The Barnstorming Days

Chet Derby is a tough old guy, the last of a dying breed of barnstorming stunt pilots. He wears a leather flyer's jacket with a cap pulled low over his eyes. Chet comes from northern California, up near Red Bluff, and makes his living as a crop duster, flying endless passes over the vast Sacramento Valley cropland.

Since the war ended, the air shows have become really popular. He can pick up a lot of extra cash stunt-flying his old biplane on weekends. He's good at it, daring and sure . . . a favorite with the crowds. He can pull out of a spin at ten feet off the deck.

This weekend, 60,000 show up at the Oakland Airport to watch the thrill-packed show—stunt-flyers, wing-walkers, daredevils, and jet bombers flying low in tight formation. The show is free, and there are plenty of thrills for the whole family. It's a sunny fall day, crisp and pleasant. Dorothy Godard, Miss Aviation of 1949, arrives to preside as queen of the air show.

The early birds sit on the bleachers with lap robes and sandwiches. The rest sit on folding chairs and boxes or just sprawl out on the paved runways. They look up at the rolls and loops for hours, trying to keep from getting a stiff neck. Some folks wander around, looking at the airplanes on display. The kids crawl inside, touching everything in the cockpit.

Among the throng of people is *Oakland Tribune* staff photographer Bill Crouch. A pilot himself, he covers this event every year. He positions himself carefully, getting good shots of Chet Derby with a wing-walker standing on his top wing, the biplane rolling and turning in the sky.

For the show's finale, Chet is flying circles in the sky, with smoke trailing behind to trace his movements. He'll be immediately followed by a low-flying formation of three air force B-29 Superfortresses, howling overhead. Only something goes wrong. The B-29s are one minute too soon!

He is at the top of his circle and coming down when they roar through him. He never even sees them . . . he's upside down. It looks like they're going right through his windshield. The crowd gasps, people standing up, pointing.

When he lands, he asks them, "How close?" They tell him, grinning, "Five feet."

It was a day to remember!

1951 The Bridge at Pyongyang

In the bitter cold winter of 1950, from the barren hills and fields of North Korea, the U.N. troops look across the Yalu River, toward the Chinese border. They have been driving north for months, pushing the North Koreans before them. But now, with the eerie clang of cymbals, hundreds of thousands of Chinese Communist soldiers pour across the border.

In the first days of December, things begin to unravel. The U.N. forces fighting in the north begin a strategic withdrawal before the Chinese hordes. By the time they get to Pyongyang, the old capital of North Korea, it has become a rout.

The U.N. forces, mostly American, stream out of the stricken city, mobbing the two small airports, pleading for "rides the hell out of here." All roads leading south are clogged with military vehicles, bumper to bumper.

The retreating forces set fires all over the city, destroying all supplies, equipment, and ammunition. The nearly deserted city is ablaze, the fires fanned by the bone-chilling wind from the north. The acrid smoke fills the sky as far as the eye can see, darkening the sun.

All civil order in the city gone, the North Korean guerrillas and the Communist underground take charge. In back alleys and along roadsides the reprisals begin against those sympathetic to the Korean Republic. Small arms fire can be heard by the retreating soldiers. Many, many civilians are fleeing their homes in fear, taking what they can carry. They have become the most pitiful victims of war, the refugees.

They follow behind the soldiers, keeping just ahead of the Communists as they sweep south all the way from the Manchurian border. The smoke and the terrible smell of death follow both armies.

Along the banks of the Taedong River, thousands of refugees gather. They must cross the river to escape south. The only way . . . a treacherous, bombed-out bridge. The ugly, twisted girders dangle over the icy water as they start across.

They look like ants as they crawl over the mangled steel. A bitter cold wind coming down from Siberia pushes against them as they crawl, inch by inch, up and down the girders. The bridge is iced over. Their hands freeze to the steel. They are mostly poor peasants, homeless and scared, not guerrillas or politicos. They are in agony as they inch along, slowly, slowly. Many slip into the icy water.

Among the soldiers who have already crossed over on pontoon bridges up river, one man looks back, Max Desfor, a correspondent and news photographer for Associated Press. A veteran of war, he has been on the front lines since the beginning. "Hardened as I was to war, this is the most heart-rending sight I've seen."

With two pairs of gloves to keep his hands from freezing, he climbs out on the jagged pieces of the bombed-out bridge. Below him is a sheer drop of fifty feet. He records the moment, whispering to himself, "Those poor, miserable souls."

Thousands of refugees on the shore are waiting in the sub-zero weather for their chance to crawl across the bridge. Bundled against the cold as best they can, they huddle with their miserable belongings. Those lucky enough to finally get across, wearily trudge south.

Beyond the river, they still have a long way to go.

1953 Adlai Bares His Sole

1952. Candidate Adlai sets out to talk to the American people. He canvasses the country—East, West and, today, a Labor Day Speech in Flint, Michigan. He sees many faces, shakes many hands, eats much chicken, and spends many sleepless nights. But just how many pairs of shoes does it take to get to Washington?

He doesn't go looking for it. He is serving as Governor of Illinois, carrying on the family tradition of public service to his state that dates back to the circuit-riding days of Lincoln. A liberal reformer, he shakes up the Illinois government by axing 1,300 political hangers-on, overhauling the welfare program, transforming the police force from a bushel of political plums into a responsive squad of law enforcers, and pushing through seventy-eight bills to streamline state government.

But Truman and other party leaders come looking for him. They seek him out with determination. The Democrats line up behind Adlai, and the ball is rolling. By the time they get to the convention in Chicago, the draft-Stevenson movement is unstoppable. The Democratic National Convention has its man in one of the few genuine drafts in America's political history.

The man they have is a bit of an oddball . . . unique in the political arena of the times. Eloquence, intellect, and an aristocratic bearing are not common in the earthy Washington of "Give 'Em Hell Harry" or the fearful witch-hunting days of "Tail-Gunner Joe McCarthy." America thinks him too much the egghead, and possibly a soft egg at that—soft on Communism.

But he is a man ahead of his times, speaking the hard truth. "The ordeal of the twentieth century—the bloodiest, most turbulent era of the whole Christian age—is far from over. Sacrifice, patience, understanding and implacable purpose, may be our lot for years to come. Let's face it. Let's talk some sense to the American people. Let's tell them the truth, that there are no gains without pains, that we are now on the eve of great decisions, not easy decisions. . . ."

However, America is looking forward to laying back and taking it easy after a long battle with depression at home and Fascism abroad. There are few ears to hear of a world in unsettled transition to a new atomic age, to hear of the troubles of emerging nations.

In November, America votes for war hero Eisenhower, who promises an easier ride and quicker solutions. Adlai goes on to become a symbol of American ideals, as a diplomat, statesman, and ambassador to the United Nations.

Photographer Bill Gallagher of the *Flint Journal* is waiting in front of the speaker's platform for Stevenson, expecting a routine shot. Then the seated candidate crosses his legs, revealing a hole in his shoe. A problem: Gallagher can't sight his camera without lying on the floor and tipping Stevenson and everyone else off. "I set the camera at arm's length on the platform, hoped I would get everything and snapped the picture. I'll probably never be so lucky again the rest of my life."

In autographing the picture, Adlai wrote: "To William Gallagher, from a candidate who is really not holier than thou!"

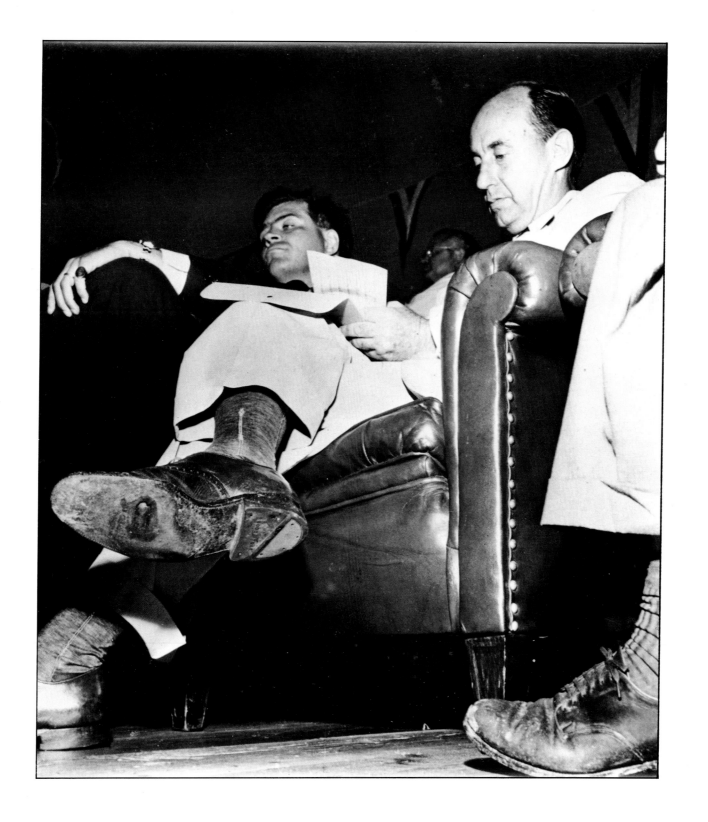

1954 A Miracle

It's a beautiful Sunday morning, sunny and warm. Walter and Virginia Schau are on a fishing trip in the Shasta Lake region near Redding, California. They crawl along behind a huge tractor-trailer, as they wind up the twisting road to the Pit River bridge. They try to pass, but there are too many turns.

In the back of the car, along with all the fishing gear, is Virginia's old Brownie camera. She has two shots left on film that is more than a year past the developing date. They will do.

Bud Overby is driving the big diesel rig. Hank Baum sits next to him. They have just switched, and Hank is tired from hours of driving. They are making the long haul from Los Angeles to Portland, carrying fruits and vegetables.

As Bud moves out onto the bridge over the river, the steering mechanism snaps. His blood runs cold as the truck careens from side to side, smashing through the steel rails and plunging over the edge.

Somehow, miraculously, the rear wheels of the cab jam under the trailer . . . it holds. The two men are standing on the windshield, looking straight down—forty feet to the rocks at the water's edge. Hank looks over at Bud, "How in the hell do we get out of this thing?"

Walter and Virginia see the truck plunge off the bridge and out of sight. They run to the edge and when they see the cab dangling there, the men trapped inside, they yell to the other cars for a rope. The man in the car behind them has a long marine rope, and Walter lowers it down, calling out, "Hey, down there, we got a rope up here, and we'll try to pull you up."

Bud Overby is closest to the window, and he grabs the rope. He turns to his buddy, "Good luck, Hank. I'll get the rope back down to you as soon as I can."

Virginia runs over to a point across from the bridge, and with the last two shots in her Brownie, she records the incredible rescue.

But the drama is not over. One man is still down there. The cab is smoking now, as burning diesel fuel trickles into the cab. Hank is leaning out the window to get enough air . . . and then the cab catches fire.

The men above are desperately trying to get him the rope. Hank reaches for it through the blinding smoke. Hanging tightly to the rope, he steps out of the cab, and is pulled from certain death.

When he gets up to the road, Overby grabs him and they hold each other, still shaking . . . "The man upstairs really had his arm around us." At that moment, the cab bursts into flame and falls, crashing down on the rocks far below.

1955 Tragedy in the Surf

A moment of obvious intensity. A couple crystallized against the invincible and overwhelming power of the sea . . . a man and a woman pitched in a drama with nature. Where is their baby?

They had spent the morning tagging the surf along Hermosa Beach—Mr. and Mrs. John McDonald—while their infant son played nearby. And then, in one moment, he is swept away by the crashing surf.

Cries of neighbors: "Something's happened on the beach!" Now they understand the anguished dance at water's edge—the desperate clutching, the aborted movements.

Jack Gaunt, *Los Angeles Times* photographer, resident of Hermosa Beach, is home this morning, not due at the *Times* until midafternoon. He hears shouts and commotion a few doors from his house. Racing toward the beach with his camera, Gaunt sights the couple from 200 feet away.

Those first moments of helplessness frozen for history on April 2, 1954.

1956 A Day in the Suburbs

In 1956, the Pulitzer Prize is won collectively by the photographers of the *New York Daily News* for their news picture coverage in 1955. Their work is a powerful display of life and death, hope and despair in a great city, twenty-four hours a day. This startling photograph by George Mattson is a part of that story.

November 2, 1955 . . . Mattson is flying in the *Daily News* plane out in the suburbs of Long Island. As they fly over East Meadow, he looks down at the rows and rows of manicured homes. The houses look a little unreal, they're so perfect and uniform. Seeing a cloud of smoke in the distance, he turns to the pilot: "Let's take a look."

As they circle over, he can't believe what he sees. A huge B-26 has crashed in the middle of the block without hitting any houses . . . not even a telephone pole. The plane is burning in someone's front yard. The right engine is sitting on the doorstep; the other is in the driveway.

The pilots, Captain Clayton Elwood and Sergeant Charles Slater, were returning to Mitchell Field when something went wrong with their propellers. They fought the controls as the plane began to lose altitude. They missed Meadowbrook Hospital by 500 feet.

The plane smashed to the ground, showering the block with fiery shrapnel, igniting the house and a car. The pilots are both killed, but no one else is injured.

It is a lucky day in the suburbs.

1957 The *Andrea Doria*

Out on the open sea there are no highways, no signs or boundaries neatly laid out. Just a vast, trackless body of water. Man relies on sophisticated radar equipment when he can't see . . . in the storms, the night, and the fog.

On the dark night of July 25, 1956, there is a dense fog off the Nantucket coast. That's not unusual. The weather in the North Atlantic is often harsh. Two great ships are heading toward each other.

The *Andrea Doria* is on the last leg of the nine-day voyage from her home port of Genoa, Italy. In the morning, she will dock at New York City. The *Andrea Doria* is possibly the most beautiful ocean liner afloat. She reflects Italy's heritage of elegant design.

Works of art are lavishly displayed . . . murals, ceramic mosaics, crystals, panels of rare wood. Each class of accommodations has its own theatre with daily movies, each its own swimming pool. She is the ultimate in luxury.

The *Stockholm* has just left New York this morning. She is heading directly toward the *Andrea Doria.* For an ocean liner, the *Stockholm* is relatively small, but she is comfortable and fast. She is lean and sleek, like a racing yacht. And she has a massive, heavy-duty steel reinforced bow for plowing through ice fields.

The captains of both ships watch each other on the radar . . . just small blips moving closer together. The radar tells them that they will pass safely, more than a mile apart. But, when they look out into the fog, each captain swears that the other ship suddenly turns directly into his path. The mystery is never fully explained.

In the warm comfort of the *Andrea Doria,* Tom Gramigni, a candy maker from Hershey, Pennsylvania, is having a nightcap at the bar. He glances out the window and is startled to see what "looks like a city all lit up . . ." moving down on them. It is 11:21.

At 11:22, the sleeping passengers are wakened by a hideous tearing sound, and they see the grayish white hulk which is the bow of the *Stockholm* passing by them in their rooms. Many are crushed instantly.

Sparks fly, as steel rips through steel, driven by 14,600 horsepower engines. In a matter of minutes, 240,000 gallons of sea water gush into the nearly empty fuel tanks, causing the *Andrea Doria* to list over on her side.

Other than her completely crumpled bow, the *Stockholm* is all right. But the lovely *Andrea Doria* is mortally wounded. The gash is forty feet wide; the *Stockholm* penetrates one-third of the way through her.

Immediately, an S.O.S. is broadcast across the ocean, and ships from all directions come to the rescue with lifeboats. Because the *Andrea Doria* is listing so badly, half her own lifeboats are under water. The people cling to each other for support.

Down below, the corridors and rooms are a nightmare of oil, smoke, debris, and bodies. The flooding water swirls waist-deep. People with torn clothes, or no clothes at all, are frantically searching for their families. Many are weeping, some in joy, some in sorrow. Dulled by shock and exhaustion, the children are crying. People come back to their rooms to find their families and, when they open the door, there is only the open black sea.

Ships of all kinds steam out of the darkness to help. Out of the tragedy evolves the greatest sea rescue of our time. Of the 1,706 passengers on the *Andrea Doria,* only 46 lose their lives. Because of sharks in the area, no bodies are ever found.

The next morning, the *Andrea Doria* lays on her side, half submerged, all alone. Overhead, in a plane, photographer Harry Trask from the *Boston Herald-Traveler,* records her last moments. "It was a sad farewell."

At 10:09, she gives a sudden heave. Like a dying giant, she rolls over, her gigantic propeller rising up. She is giving up the struggle. With the swirl and roar of foamy water, she sinks. Once below the surface, she moves slowly and silently down, 225 feet, settling gently on the bottom. She still lies there, in exactly that position . . . as if waiting.

1958 But, Sir, the Dragon

Allen Weaver is in a world of his own . . . a world much more fascinating than this Washington, D.C., street. Masks of red and yellow and every other color of the rainbow. Fish-shaped kites and paper tigers are alive on this very street today. There is even the great Chinese dragon—a commanding sight, as it twists and turns—sprinkling its magic wherever it raises its mighty head. Fireworks trail flashes of color and light through the air.

All this charms Allen, and, like a spirit mesmerized, he moves toward the street show, drawn to the marvelous creatures. He has never seen such a street before. He must explore it.

Snaking through Maurice Cullinane's Chinatown beat is the Hip Sing Chinese Merchants Association parade. A sea of faces watches from the curb. Suddenly, the cop's reflexes quicken. From the corner of his eye, he sees a small figure stepping out into the open . . . into the path of exploding firecrackers and oncoming traffic. In that instant, their worlds meet. The young adventurer finds himself staring at two long, tall pillars of blue. The cop finds his vision cut down to half size.

It is a special moment, a moment shared between them— the child and the cop. They both have a job to do, but the doing of it takes some small measure of friendly compromise. Captured is a summit meeting of sorts, a gentle meeting of wills.

Photographer Bill Beall sees the moment and instinctively clicks. The picture draws more response than any photo ever published in the *Washington Daily News*.

1959 All the Bright, Shiny Dreams

The neighborhood at Riverside Drive and South Twenty-seventh Street in Minneapolis is utterly middle-American. You can almost feel that hazy innocence of the 1950s, everyone doggedly pursuing the American dream. All the bright, shiny-finned cars—and everything getting bigger and better. It is Friday, May 16, in this heartland of America, a little after noon—12:20 to be exact. Today will be Minnesota's most deadly traffic day in 1958 . . . fourteen people will die; one will die right on this corner.

Nine-year-old Ralph Fossum is pulling his red wagon off the curb into the busy street. It's lunchtime; school is out.

A huge dump truck is coming down the street, doing its normal, everyday job. It's still a few blocks away.

Bill Seaman, staff photographer for the *Minneapolis Star-Tribune,* is pulling up to the light at the corner. He is on roving assignment in a *Star* radio car. He sees the boy step into the street. "I was about to shout a warning to him and even considered getting out and helping him, but he made it back to the curb all right, so I drove on." The dump truck is now a block behind him.

Ralph waits impatiently a few moments and then steps into the street. He never sees the truck. Three blocks past the intersection, Bill hears on the radio that a boy has been killed by a truck at the corner of Riverside Drive and South Twenty-seventh Street. "I knew then . . ."

1960 Courtyard at San Severino

Late New Year's Eve, January 1, 1959 . . . Batista finally hightails it out of Cuba, and Havana erupts into a scene of wild celebration. Castro and his *Barbudos,* "The Bearded Ones," come down from the mountains, after years of guerrilla fighting . . . in triumph.

From Santiago de Cuba, he begins his 600-mile trip to Havana, stopping in every little town and village. The people are dancing in the streets. For more than a week, Castro and his men are showered with affection, riding through triumphant celebrations all across Cuba. The people love to hear him speak in his lyrical way, and they gather around him wherever he goes.

Correspondents from all over the world pour into Havana. They are given credentials by Fidel that allow them to go anywhere they wish. Andy Lopez, a veteran news photographer for United Press International, covers the war crimes tribunal at Matanzas, forty miles from Havana.

The San Severino Castle at Matanzas was a military base for the Batista army. There is a huge moat around the castle, twenty feet wide. To get into the castle, you have to cross a lowered bridge. Hundreds of people want to get into the trial to testify against a brutal Batista army corporal, José Rodriguez, nicknamed "Pepe Caliente." They hate Pepe in the worst way. So many people try to get across the bridge that at least fifty fall into the moat.

"The trial room was small, thirty or forty feet across. The place was jammed with people . . . it was hot and sweaty. People were climbing all over the tables, drinking Coca-Colas and throwing cigars on the floor. It was incredible.

"The Prosecutor was Willy Galvez, the twenty-five-year-old military commander of Matanzas and a rebel major. At one point Willy turned to Pepe and said, 'When we get through with you, Pepe Caliente ("Hot Pete"), they're going to call you Pepe Frio ("Cold Pete").'

"There was a noisy public address system hooked up outside so everyone could hear. The entire trial took two hours. . . . It took one minute for the three tribunal judges to condemn Pepe to death.

"I was there when they lined Pepe against the wall in the courtyard. He dropped to his knees, and a priest came over to give him religious comfort and last rites. Pepe reached over to kiss the cross before he was to be executed. It was a tragic moment, and I took their picture.

"Suddenly, Willy Galvez came over screaming at me, poking me in the chest, telling me I can't take pictures. I was standing there arguing with him, and in the background I could see eight or nine *Barbudos,* who were waiting for all this to come to an end so they could get on with their business and shoot this guy. They had all different kinds of hats and uniforms—a cowboy hat, a U.S. Army hat, straw hats, berets, jeans, Army fatigues—all different.

"Finally, Galvez said, 'I'll have that film.' So I said, 'O.K., and took a roll of film out of my pocket. I gave it to him and they let us go. I kept the roll of film with Pepe on it."

After Lopez is gone, they put Pepe against the wall. Just before they fire, Willy Galvez stops the execution, stating that the tribunal has not yet given the official order. Pepe is executed the next day, January 18, 1959.

1961 Politics by Sword

The eighteenth-century samurai warriors, much like America's Western marshals, traveled Japan's countryside, enforcing their own code of honor and duty. They reached beyond the arm of established law; they were their own law. Masters with the sword, the samurai took vengeance on the "dishonorable" with pride and patriotic zeal. The samurai concept of honorable violence runs deep.

A crowd of 3,000 Japanese citizens packs Tokyo's Hibiya Hall for the three-party political debates that launch the campaign for parliamentary elections next month. Yasushi Nagao, staff photographer for the newspaper *Mainichi,* is covering the event, along with live television crews and other photographers. He's been here for a while, listening to the political leaders. Standing only fifteen feet from the speaker's platform, Nagao has a clear view and has already burned up all but one frame of film.

Taking the speaker's podium is Socialist Party Chairman Inejiro Asanuma. A gruff man, heavy-set and gravel-voiced, he blasts the Liberal Democratic party and the Japanese-U.S. security pact. Only minutes into his speech, heckling and jeers break out from a group of rightist students who have taken over a section of the front row. "Down with the stooge of Peking!" Asanuma pauses to wait out the commotion, but then continues in spite of the student protests. Photographers rush toward the uproar, but Nagao has only one remaining shot. He waits.

A slight figure darts—catlike—onto the stage from the opposite side of the hall, carrying what looks like a brown stick. He charges toward Asanuma, who is behind the speaker's rostrum, with such force that the politician's papers go flying in all directions.

As Asanuma turns to face the onrushing seventeen-year-old university student, the youth plunges a foot-long sword eleven inches into his abdomen. He gasps, wincing. The student withdraws the bloodied weapon, and Asanuma staggers out from behind the podium—in audience view for the first time.

Now, again . . . a second thrust . . . into his chest. Photographer Nagao stands just to the side of the rostrum. With his last piece of film, he shoots as the student withdraws the blade from his second thrust. Asanuma totters, then drops to the floor in a heap. He dies before reaching the hospital two blocks away.

Otoya Yamaguchi, an ultranationalist with a prior record of nine arrests for violence, assassinates Asanuma as a "pro-Communist enemy of the people." A political zealot, he acts as an agent of honor with staunch indifference to the consequences. He later commits suicide.

On October 12, 1960, assassination by sword is no longer just a memory of Japan's feudal past.

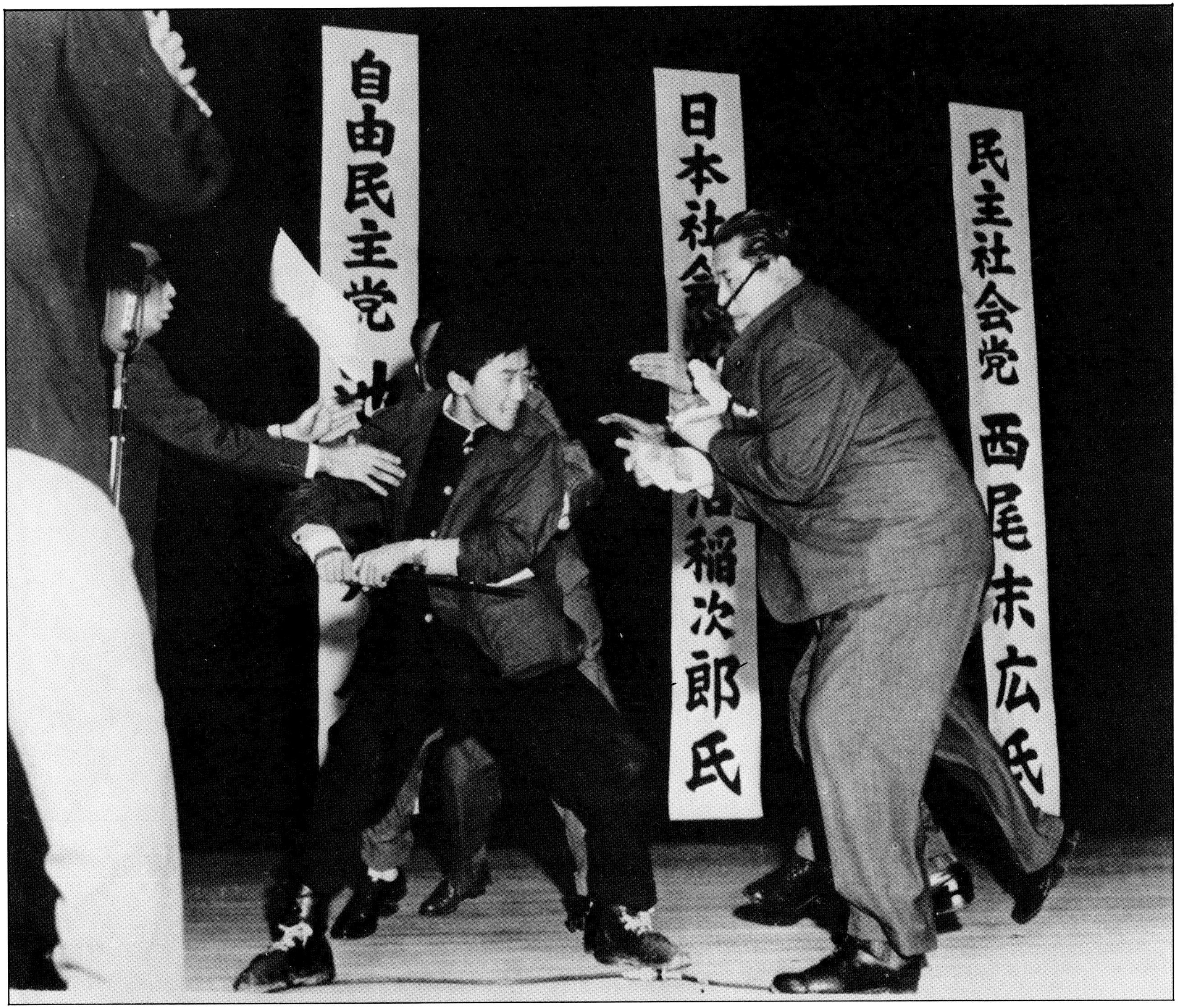
自由民主党
日本社
稲次郎氏
民主社会党
西尾末広氏

1962 The Birth of the Sixties

April 22, 1961. It is a chilly, overcast day at Camp David. Last year's leaves are still piled around. The trees are barren.

Here, at the presidential mountain retreat in Maryland, JFK has asked to meet with Ike, in an effort to come to grips with the Bay of Pigs fiasco. Only three months in office, Kennedy has a world crisis on his hands. He needs help. He turns to the old man.

They pose for a few shots with the press, and then Ike turns to the young man and says, "Come on up here, I know a place where we can talk."

The photographers turn away, all except one. Paul Vathis, AP photographer, watches them as they walk away. "There were just the two of them, all by themselves, their heads bowed, walking up the path. They looked so lonely . . . "

The weather is moody and threatening . . . and so are the times. This is the birth of the sixties.

The Eisenhower years were placid and innocent . . . news about him usually came from the golf course. But in 1961, the whole American scene is changing, and John Kennedy is a big part of it. Here is the young president for the young mood. Children's toys litter the White House . . . touch football on the lawn . . . movie stars, starlight and glamour . . . Camelot.

America is on the move, looking outward to change the world. Young people are expanding their horizons, a new spirit is on the land. Young America becomes the exporter of freedom and democracy in all lands . . . the policeman of the world.

It was like Camelot before the Crusades.

1963 Final Absolution

Political upheaval . . . a part of life in South America. Here, in Venezuela in 1962, there have already been two other uprisings—both unsuccessful. Less than one month after the last insurrection at Carupano is squelched, the dissatisfied politicos rise again at Puerto Cabello Naval Base, sixty miles from Caracas.

Puerto Cabello has seen its share of fighting. Years ago, marauding pirates combed the Venezuelan coastal towns in search of gold and silver treasure. Puerto Cabello was designed by the Spanish to withstand these attacks. But this time the attack comes from within. A military coup, played out on these ancient rocky streets.

Dawn . . . 500 rebel marines seize the naval base. Within the hour they control the whole town of Puerto Cabello as well. President Romulo Betancourt's new constitutional government is threatened.

In Caracas, the press corps snaps into high gear. They have already left when photographer Hector Rondon reports for work, so he rushes after them, to Puerto Cabello.

Government forces gather quickly and overwhelm the base. Tanks, mobile artillery, and troops move into the town, pushing ahead in a savage ten-block drive. Rondon arrives—and advances—with the troops, crouching behind a tank as he goes.

"I found myself in solid lead for forty-five minutes. I was flattened against the wall, while the bullets were flying, when the priest appeared. The truth is, I don't know how I took those pictures. Lying on the ground, I just began shooting pictures while the bullets were whistling."

There is no place to hide. Sabre jets run strafing attacks from the air and fierce fighting cuts up the street in brutal door-to-door combat. Peasants from the surrounding mountains, armed with machetes, join with the loyalists.

Father Luis Padilla, navy chaplain at the base, is much needed today. Many lie dying in the streets. He moves among the wounded, doing his job—administering the Sacrament. A dying loyalist creeps toward him on bended knee, clinging to him for strength. Rebel sniper fire slices through the air.

"I looked up at the sniper with the submachine gun in the window. He kept shooting, spraying the street around me. The street was full of flying lead. As the soldier was dying I gave him absolution."

Loyalists move from door to door, trading lives for inches in the rebel-held sector. The leftist forces, confined to a four-block area, are losing ground as loyalists flush them out. By nightfall, the surviving rebels escape into the mountains.

The two-day revolt leaves over 200 dead and 1,000 wounded. Father Padilla has absolved a multitude of sins today. Venezuela is quiet . . . for a time.

Live . . . from Dallas

Bob Jackson, photographer for the *Dallas Times Herald,* is dead tired as he waits in the basement of the city jail for Lee Harvey Oswald to be brought out. Only forty-seven hours earlier, he had been sitting in the back of a convertible behind President Kennedy's motorcade. He heard three shots, looked up at where they were coming from and saw the assassin's rifle being drawn back into the window. He has not slept much since.

Now they are moving Oswald from the city jail to the county jail, from one end of town to another. It is a normal procedure. They feel he will be safer there. Also, they are under pressure from the networks to allow Oswald to be televised. They want a picture of this guy . . . everyone wants to see him. It is the biggest news story going . . . and it's live!

An anonymous telephone call to the FBI at 2:15 A.M. the night before warned that Oswald would be killed during the transfer from the city lockup to the county jail. The FBI immediately relayed the warning to both city and county police. Later, the city police dispatcher said that call never came in.

Bob Jackson: "I had seen Ruby once. He came up to the photo department at the paper and brought one of his strippers up there who danced with a snake. He was getting publicity for her.

"Ruby loved the police. He owned a striptease club, and he always wanted to keep on their good side. He would go up to the police station late at night, bring them sandwiches and hang around, like a buddy."

As Bob is waiting with the other newsmen and camera crews, they announce that Oswald is being brought down. "In the air was the feeling that something could happen. When Oswald came out the door, I raised the camera to my eye. People yelled out, 'Here he comes' . . . I was ready.

"We stood in a semicircle about eleven feet in front of the door which formed a little clearing. I was leaning against the fender of a police car. As I looked through the camera, Oswald took eight or ten steps, and I saw a body moving into my line of sight. I leaned over the car to the left. Ruby moved three quick steps and bang. When he shot, I shot."

History turns on crucial moments, and Jackson's photograph freezes this one. It records the instant the bullet entered Oswald's body. His face contorts as he clutches his chest . . . the bullet fired by a man who wasn't supposed to be there. And millions of Americans watch it happen live, sitting in their living rooms.

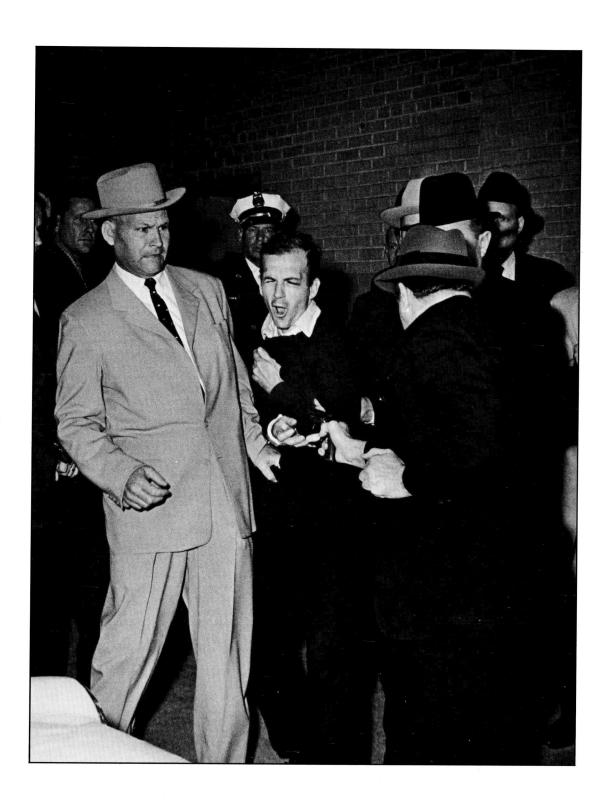

1965 and 1966

A War Like No Other

Out of the mire of the French Indochina conflict of the forties and fifties comes the Vietnam War of the sixties. The French are confounded by a lack of support from the villagers; the United States is destined to learn about that, too. For eight years, the French continue, with U.S. aid increasing each year, but are overtaken at Dienbienphu in 1954. What is left, we inherit . . . a land of unresolved conflicts, lingering tensions, and a demoralized populace.

It starts with a smattering of military advisers, arms and equipment during the later Eisenhower years. Through the Kennedy administration, the number of advisory personnel grows, as the Vietcong sabotage units and infiltration campaigns into the South increase. Now, in the mid-sixties, America is up to her neck in a war that sneaked up on her, leaving few choices—and much responsibility.

It is a time when American politicians think of Asian nations as so many dominoes: One nation falling to communism will cause a chain reaction. South Vietnam and all of Southeast Asia must be defended against the encroaching arm of communism. The United States, assuming the role of world defender of democracy, moves into Vietnam full force, escalating ground and air support tremendously. By the end of 1965, there are 180,000 U.S. troops in Vietnam as compared to 23,000 the year before.

The American buildup changes the face of Vietnam—its landscape and its people. Millions of yards of land are leveled and paved over for airfields. Thousands of miles of road are constructed and seaports are carved out. Civic-action programs take on the job of persuading the people that the Saigon government is worth supporting. These special envoys focus on building up local services and defenses, constructing bridges and barbed-wire fences around the villages, digging wells, dispensing medicine, training hamlet militias. The effectiveness of civic action efforts are dubious. The population remains as distrustful as ever of the government.

Destruction is a way of life for the Vietnamese. Countless villages are caught in crossfire. The homeless stand like ghosts on the horizon . . . their huts burned, their crops destroyed, their lives uncertain.

These are some of the images captured by veteran combat photographers Horst Faas of the Associated Press and Kyoichi Sawada of United Press International. A Vietnamese mother and her children wade across a river to escape bombs raining from U.S. aircraft during a strike on their village. The Vietcong's use of their village as a base to fire on U.S. Marines is a bad omen. They know their home will be gone forever.

A Vietnamese father holds his child, her body completely covered with burns from a napalm bomb, after a strafing attack on their village. Vietcong guerrillas were hiding there among the villagers. The child is found in a field of reeds.

A Vietnamese Special Forces Unit, bristling with weapons, carries a comrade wounded by an exploding mine.

Death comes by the cartload here.

Faas and Sawada get their pictures the hard way, by following ground action in isolated outposts, flying helicopter missions in pursuit of guerrillas, narrowly escaping death in mine fields, rice paddies, and jungle brush. Of Faas, Brigadier General Cao Van Vien says, "That's the luckiest man alive. He'll never know how close he came to being killed." Later, Sawada is killed in Cambodia—October 28, 1970—his blood-stained press card found near his body. He dies in the same area of Cambodia where he was captured six months before.

It is a war like no other, a war without front lines . . . elusive, yet ever-present, stubbornly persistent. A war of ambushes and booby-traps in the dark, overgrown recesses of the jungle and the leech-laden waters of the steamy marshes. America's idea was to move into Vietnam, take the situation in hand, and sweep out in one swift, victorious push. We never expected it to be so long, so hard.

60

1967 Welcome to Mississippi

There had been thunder when they last met—James Meredith and Ole Miss. Fall of 1962. Meredith becomes the first black person to enter the University of Mississippi, a bold-fisted challenge to discriminatory admissions policies in America's colleges.

Meredith's challenge meets a storm of resistance—rioting, killings. So much so that Meredith is under constant federal guard during his time at the university. With his graduation in 1963, the two-year duel lapses. But Mississippi would remember.

June 6, 1967. Meredith is coming home after time in Africa and New York's Columbia Law School. Home to Mississippi . . . on foot, walking alone and unarmed through some of the most remote and racially unsettled counties in the state. It is a 220-mile stretch from Memphis, Tennessee, to Jackson, Mississippi. He is making his solitary journey to promote black voter registration and to combat the fears blacks feel about living and traveling freely in Mississippi.

"My objective was to expose the all-pervasive fear that existed. You had a million blacks in Mississippi, 12,000 registered to vote. Now, this was two years after Johnson had signed the Voting Rights Bill, but still no one had registered to vote. Even though Johnson had signed a bill saying that blacks have the right to vote and all they had to do was go and sign the book, most blacks still didn't sign the book. Now, it wasn't because they didn't want to. It was because they were afraid of the consequences. They didn't know what would happen. Before, when they tried to push the point, someone would come out on the courthouse lawn and shoot them. They didn't know for sure whether there would be the same consequences, The question was—had we changed or hadn't we changed?"

Memphis, only twelve miles from Mississippi and once a giant kingpin of the cotton empire, is the starting point. People are attracted to his mission. A black soldier, a Memphis businessman, a minister from New York spontaneously take up the march with him—all on the basis of an inspiring chance meeting.

Meredith is a compelling figure, helmeted, carrying an ebony and ivory walking stick, a gift from an African tribal chieftain. He walks past the hopeful and the hate-filled.

Occasional groups of blacks dot the roadside with quiet support and prayers, even as cars full of angry whites dog him along Highway 51, wildly swerving in his direction. It is a continual intimidation. Threats of blind anger pour out. "I hope to hell you die before you get there." He walks on.

It is a hot, sultry afternoon. The heat shimmers above the steamy asphalt highway. Photographer Jack Thornell is covering the march for Associated Press. "We were leapfrogging with our cars, just staying a little ahead of him."

From the bushes a man's voice speaks quietly: "James. James. I only want James Meredith." Meredith turns toward the voice in the bushes, and gunshot ricochets along the road. The other marchers sprawl out on the highway.

"What alerted us was the first shot. I think it was a warning shot to scare everyone else away. I hopped out of the car and started taking pictures."

Now, two successive blasts shatter the stillness. Meredith falls, writhing on the asphalt. From the brush skirting Highway 51, a man is apprehended, whom neighbors describe as a "very nice man—as nice a neighbor as you could ask for."

Meredith is rushed to a Memphis hospital. Emergency surgery will carve sixty shotgun pellets from his head, neck, back, and legs.

For his deadly assault on James Meredith, Aubrey James Norvell will spend eighteen months in jail.

Dr. Martin Luther King, Stokely Carmichael, Dick Gregory, and other black leaders continue the march. By the time they get to Jackson they are 18,000 strong. The march will give rise to a new force and a new phrase . . . "Black Power."

(The attacker is actually visible in the top photograph, his head and chest rising from the embankment to the left of Meredith, who is looking back at his assailant.)

1968 Kiss of Life

A routine summer morning in Jacksonville, Florida—warm, muggy, overcast. No surprises. Everything moving along normally . . . except for some hubbub over in one of the suburbs. The power has been knocked out, leaving air conditioners idle and residents grouchy.

The crew has a big job ahead—get the juice flowing again. Jim Thompson, Randall Champion, and the rest climb their poles and belt themselves into position.

"I was on assignment when I passed the men working on the overhead power lines." Rocco Morabito, staff photographer on the *Jacksonville Journal,* makes a mental note to snap some photographs of them on the way back.

The fact is, all the lines *are* dead—except one. That single live wire finds Champion . . . the life is literally jolted out of him. He is left dangling upside down, blue, and unconscious. His buddies know in an instant: How the charge can blaze right through a body, leaving holes where the electricity burns out. How there is so little time.

All along the block, they scramble down the poles, racing toward Champion. Their stricken buddy is hanging in limbo between life and death. It is the kind of moment that draws an extraordinary measure of strength from an otherwise ordinary life.

Jim Thompson reaches the pole first and scales it. Clutching Champion close, mouth upon mouth, he begins pumping air into his friend's lungs. Slowly, steadily, coaxing life back into his body.

Morabito returns at this moment, sees the emergency, and radios for help. Then he takes his picture. The others can only wait.

They all hold still in that long moment, hoping for a sign of life.

"He's breathing," Jim whispers.

It was a sweet kiss . . . the kiss of life.

1968 Feature
Dreams of Better Times

Dreams and friends . . . a soldier doesn't have much more out here . . . maybe a poncho, a mosquito net, and a rifle. But it is the dreams and the friendships that keep him sane in Vietnam.

An unnamed American GI is sleeping through the monsoon rains, as a buddy watches guard. Here, you take your moments of peace wherever you find them. For the time being, there is no war, no monsoon season, no wading knee-deep through swamps and flooded rice paddies, no mud. Gone are the specters of the wounded in pain and agony, waiting hours for medical attention, and the wandering refugees in need of everything. A temporary reprieve from the nagging feeling of being watched from the jungle brush. His buddy is taking care of all that for a while.

He sleeps, wrapped in his poncho, for protection from the rain. The versatile poncho keeps the warmth in, and the dampness and the red ants out. And, in case of injury, a soldier wrapped in a poncho can be dragged out of terrain in which a stretcher could not maneuver.

A combat photographer for United Press International, Toshio Sakai, catches the GI as he dreams of better times.

This year, 1968, is the first time the Pulitzer Prize is awarded in two categories, spot news and feature. Both pictures speak the same language—one man caring for another. It is a heartening set of images . . . a breather in times of trouble.

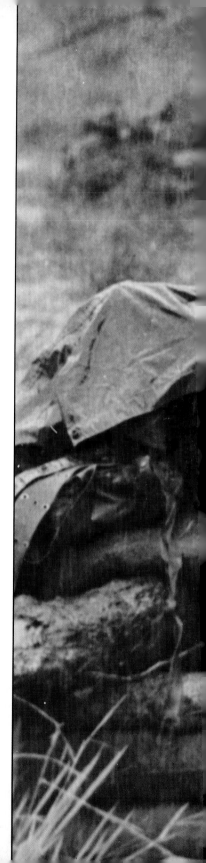

1969 Democracy and Freedom?

Vietnam . . . it's like a bad dream we just can't shake. As the small number of economic advisers increases over the years and eventually is replaced by hundreds of thousands of fighting men, America comes to feel the tremendous drain. What starts as a part-time sore spot becomes an unending nightmare.

In 1968, the Vietcong mount their massive Tet offensive. War rages in the streets of Saigon. It is early afternoon, February 1, in the Cholon district of the city.

AP photographer, Eddie Adams, is out on the streets, covering the fighting. He comes upon a scene that grabs him and won't let go. From a distance, Adams sees a group of Vietnamese Marines and police escorting a man whose hands are tied behind his back. He is the suspected leader of a Vietcong commando unit.

Adams trails them as they slip around a corner, leaving the open combat zone. The prisoner is pushed along in a forced walk to an awaiting police jeep. Brigadier General Nguyen Ngoc Loan, Vietnam's national police chief, emerges from behind the jeep with his bone-handled revolver. He doesn't have much time . . . just enough for a quick back-street execution. The police step back. Now, it is only the general and the prisoner.

Loan moves directly toward the prisoner. Adams waits in the background, not knowing what will happen next. Suddenly, Loan raises his revolver to within inches of the captive's head . . . and fires.

"Loan gave no indication that he was to shoot the prisoner until he did it. As his hand came up with the revolver, so did my camera, but I still didn't expect him to shoot. When he fired, I fired."

The general puts his gun back into his belt, and the body completes its fall.

In one split second . . . the whole rotten war stares us down, smashing any naive notions of good guys and bad guys. A picture of the stark naked truth of Vietnam, without the ideals and the justifications. The doubts and suspicions grow. Is this the democracy and freedom we're defending?

1969 Feature
I've Been to the Mountaintop

" . . . and if you're around when I have to meet my day, I don't want a long funeral. And if you get somebody to deliver the eulogy, tell him not to talk too long."

Martin Luther King, Jr., is dead, struck down as he stepped out onto his motel balcony in Memphis. On the evening of April 4, 1968, a bullet fired from the gun of James Earl Ray came crashing into his neck as his friends Reverend Ralph Abernathy and Reverend Jesse Jackson stood close by. The disciple of nonviolence . . . cut down by a high-powered rifle.

It is difficult to deliver a short eulogy for this monumental man. Over the years since the Montgomery bus boycott in 1955, he was the untiring moral crusader . . . defending the rights of the poor and oppressed against unjust practices. His techniques: nonviolent civil disobedience and passive resistance.

He became the national symbol of the civil rights movement. It all started in Montgomery, Alabama, with the bus boycott to force desegregated seating on the city's buses and continued with the sit-ins to integrate public facilities—lunch counters, hotels, theatres, department stores, and then, on to voter-registration marches.

The funeral service is held at Ebenezer Baptist Church in Atlanta, his pulpit for the last eight years. His familiar black congregation shares the small sanctuary today with a sea of recognizable government leaders—Hubert Humphrey, Robert Kennedy, Jacqueline Kennedy, senators, Supreme Court justices, United Nations officials. They come to mourn his passing along with his widow, Coretta Scott King, and their children.

Photographer for *Ebony* magazine, Moneta Sleet, Jr., has his position inside the church, after some difficulty getting clearance through security lines. "Everyone was highly emotional and still in shock over the suddenness of his death. There was all kinds of tension. They were still looking for the killer, and the guards around the church were mainly white state troopers who the blacks had been confronting all these years." Coretta King looks down to comfort her daughter, Bernice. Moneta takes their photograph.

In the end, King's own words are eulogy enough:

The March on Washington, 1963: "I have a dream that one day this nation will rise up and live out the true meaning of its creed: 'We hold these truths to be self-evident, that all men are created equal.' I have a dream that one day, on the red hills of Georgia, the sons of former slaves and the sons of former slave owners will be able to sit down together at the table of brotherhood. I have a dream that one day even the State of Mississippi, a state sweltering with the people's injustice, sweltering with the heat of oppression, will be transformed into an oasis of freedom and justice. I have a dream that my four little children will one day live in a nation where they will not be judged by the color of their skin but by the content of their character. I have a dream that one day every valley shall be exalted, every hill and mountain shall be made low, the rough places will be made plain, and the crooked places will be made straight, and the glory of the Lord shall be revealed and all flesh shall see it together."

Montgomery, Alabama, 1955: "If you will protest courageously, and yet with dignity and Christian love, when the history books are written in future generations, the historians will have to pause and say, 'There lived a great people—a black people—who injected new meaning and dignity into the veins of civilization.' This is our challenge and our overwhelming responsibility."

Memphis, Tennessee, 1968, the day before he was killed: "We've got some difficult days ahead. But it really doesn't matter with me now. Because I've been to the mountaintop. I won't mind. Like anybody, I would like to live a long life. Longevity has its place. But I'm not concerned about that now. I just want to do God's will. And he's allowed me to go up to the mountain. And I've looked over, and I've seen the Promised Land. I may not get there with you, but I want you to know tonight that we as a people will get to the Promised Land. So, I'm happy tonight. I'm not fearing any man. Mine eyes have seen the glory of the coming of the Lord."

1970 Guns in the Ivory Tower

Students of the late sixties swell in protest against the System. Jim Crow, Vietnam, Richard Nixon . . . always good for starters. Taking their learning out of the classrooms and into the streets, the irate young challenge and question in an age that itches for change.

The Establishment is vast and unreachable—a numb Goliath. A sparring partner is needed and the Movement is born. The Movement—equally inaccessible, ubiquitous—a collection of diverse interests united chiefly by a common dissatisfaction with the status quo. With a savvy for theatre and media, Students for a Democratic Society, Yippies, Hippies, Black Panthers, and others taunt the Goliath . . . and shock the deaf and blind giant into action.

In 1969, college campuses across the nation break out in turmoil, making a stand against America's participation in the war, her imperialism, the familial ties between universities and the military-industrial complex, irrelevant academic curricula, pollution, poverty, and the longtime thorn of racial injustice.

There have been problems all year at Cornell—even cross-burnings. Ghetto blacks, selected for the special Black Studies Program, claim discrimination, particularly by the fraternities. On Parents' Weekend, the pressure cooker explodes. The blacks take over the Student Union, holding the campus in an uncertain grip for two days.

AP photographer Steve Starr, aware of the significance of the story, drives from Albany to Cornell—250 miles. "I'd been up that night trying to stay on top of the story and the university public relations people were trying to keep us away from the story. It was a very up-tight situation.

"I had heard rumors that they had armed themselves and, frankly, had discounted it. I thought it was just absurd, no way that could have possibly happened. I thought it would be intriguing from a news standpoint if it had, but I didn't believe it, 'cause I hadn't seen it. I had seen one student, I thought, at a window with a gun and I thought *one* student with *one* gun was really incredible.

"It was this cold, rainy afternoon, about three o'clock, when we got the word from the university's PR people that the blacks would probably give up and come out.

"A hush fell over the crowd. The door opened, and I felt a cold chill. The blacks came out with all these rifles, shotguns, knives, homemade spears, and bandoliers, and I thought My God! I knew damn well that armed students on a campus had not occurred before and that the picture was historical.

"I shot off all the film in the camera as they came out. I was concerned that the students would start throwing rocks at me and that the blacks would open fire. There was a very definite possibility they would open fire—no melodrama, no bullshit—and I was directly in the middle of the whole thing."

Even as they surrender the building in the late afternoon of April 20, a mood of apprehension hangs in the air. Students shouldering guns and ammo on ivy-covered Cornell University . . . a prelude of things to come in the ivory tower.

1970 Feature
Migration to Misery

From the highway you can't see them. They are hidden from sight, out behind the trees. It is out there in the fields that the migrant workers' lives are thrown away . . . spent in misery, squalor, and shame—to keep the fruits and vegetables we buy in the supermarkets a few cents cheaper.

Living in wood-framed shanties, with tar paper walls, sheet metal roofs, and broken windows. Families live in ten-by-twelve-foot shacks. Children are often sick, and babies cry in hunger. And they don't even own the shacks.

You might not see them out there, but they're there. It makes it easier for us that we can't see them. That's why they're hidden. They are the forgotten people . . . our disgrace.

Against the backdrop of opulent Palm Beach County, Florida, they live, work, and die . . . in poverty. Mostly blacks from the Deep South, they move from crop to crop, across county and state lines, carrying their meager possessions in a shopping bag or cardboard box.

They begin in late January, with the Florida citrus, moving north from field to field—tomatoes and potatoes, snap beans in the Carolinas, berries and fruits in Virginia, vegetables in New Jersey and Pennsylvania, and then on to New England and Canada in the late fall. Then back to the South, to start all over.

Homeless, rootless, often unable to read or write, they cannot voice their plight. But these photographs by Dallas Kinney, of the *Palm Beach Post,* cry out the shame. "It became more than a profession . . . it became an obligation to them."

Down the rows, miles long, heads bob endlessly, the migrants stooping in the dirt all day . . . in the blazing sun, the rain, and the cold. All ages, both sexes, together. The foul black-green grease of the insecticide clings on clothes and skin, inflaming the cuts and scratches from the picking.

The migrant worker is exploited by the growers, field bosses, labor crews . . . and us. He is the bottom rung of the ladder. For a few cents a bushel, a few dollars a day, they gather our food. The rent they pay for their shacks takes most of their pay. The children, curious and bright, are soon crushed by the hopeless, dreary days of their lives.

We see them go by on the highway, in their broken-down cars and buses . . . unwanted in the towns and cities that buy their labor so cheaply.

"We live in shame because we're treated as the scum of the nation, and we live in hopelessness, for experience has shown us that there is no road open to us . . . except back to the field."

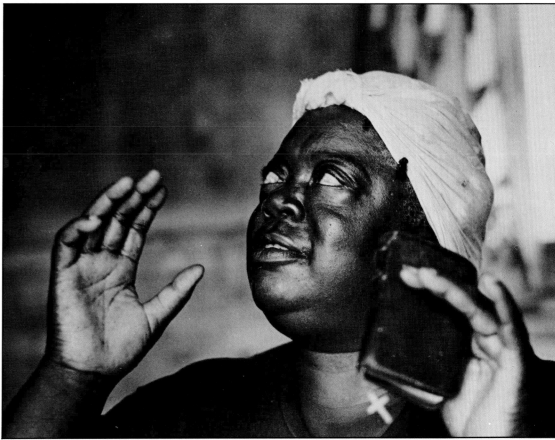

"I ain't got too much longer to wait. God's going to let me know when he gets ready for me. I'm already ready. I'm not afraid to die 'cause I'm a child of God."

Taking a rest while cooking lye soap.

1971 A God-awful Scream

John Filo: "While I was a student at Kent State, I worked as a lab technician at the School of Journalism. That Monday morning, I opened up the lab about 8:00 A.M. This was after a nasty weekend . . . not just at Kent State, but all over the country. Most colleges and universities were erupting after Nixon's announcement of the Cambodian invasion. The National Guard had been called up on Saturday after the ROTC building was burned.

"At noon, we closed the lab to go down to the rally, right outside the journalism building, Taylor Hall. When I got there, the Guard and the students had confronted each other across the Commons, about two hundred yards apart. Suddenly, there was a series of tear-gas barrages, and I was running back and forth between the two groups, taking pictures of the conflict.

"The guardsmen lined up with fixed bayonets and made a sweep across the Commons toward Taylor Hall. They didn't bother me, although I didn't give them a chance to get within striking distance of a night stick. By following them, I ended up in the parking lot behind Taylor Hall. There were about seventy-five guardsmen, helmeted and wearing black gas masks. They looked grotesque.

"After about five minutes, the Guard started moving to the top of the hill. As they were moving back, the students followed them, keeping a distance of about one hundred and fifty feet. The hostile body of the crowd was shouting and throwing rocks at the Guard. I was jogging, to get in position behind this group and the guardsmen in the background, so I could show the relationship of the two and also to be close, should anything happen.

"The Guard was moving backward, dodging rocks. As they reached the crest of the hill, they turned suddenly, dropped to one knee, and began firing directly into the crowd. People started running in all directions.

"When the firing started, the people came roaring back down the sidewalk. It was a two-foot drop from there down to the street, and, if you're running and don't expect it, you could break a leg, so I was yelling at these people, 'This is just a scare tactic.' I could see no reason for these rifles to be pointing into the crowd and firing away unless they were using blanks. I was screaming, 'Don't run, you're going to break your leg.'

"I couldn't imagine live ammunition. I was standing up, dodging back and forth, grabbing these people as they ran by me. The firing was still going on. It seemed like an awfully long time.

"I raised the camera to my eye, got it focused on the guardsmen shooting right at me. My finger is on the button, the shutter on its way down, and, at that moment, I see, over on the right side of the viewfinder, a bullet slam into a metal sculpture, going right through it and blasting a hole in a tree. The whole sculpture shook and a cloud of rust settled around it. I just dropped my camera, and said, 'My God, someone is firing real bullets.' I thought someone had made a mistake.

"Then the firing stopped. There were people laying all over the grass. I'm the only one standing up on the sidewalk. There was an officer out in front of the guardsmen with his hands up to tell them to stop shooting. As I turned around, directly over my left shoulder, I saw the body of Jeff Miller. He had been shot in the neck. It could only have been a few seconds, but already the blood was extensive, like kicking over a bucket of blood.

"With the realization that they were firing live ammunition, I said, 'This is crazy; I've got to get out of here,' and I started walking away. I think I took three steps and said, 'Wait a minute, someone's got to document this.' I turned back around. Wounded and dying people are laying all around me. Other people are pulling themselves up off the ground. No one is going near the body. And then this girl, Mary Ann Vecchio, comes running up the street and she kneels down beside the body. I started walking toward her. Her body was shaking . . . she was crying. And then she screamed—a God-awful scream. My reflexes took over, and that was it. One frame.

"After it was all over and the university was closed, I took it upon myself to just get the pictures out. The biggest thing with me was that I didn't think people would believe what had happened; it seemed so unreal. You have to understand that, at this time, I was very paranoid about what was going to happen. I didn't know if somebody was going to stop me and take my film away. I was trying to get this film into my pocket, and I was thinking about hiding it in my Volkswagen until I got to Pennsylvania. I really thought someone had blundered in killing these people, and there was going to be a mass cover-up. Already the radio reports were saying that two guardsmen and only two students were killed. Everybody was shocked at the false reports . . . they weren't telling what really happened.

"As I was driving to Pennsylvania, I began to wonder if I really had the photographs or not. I said to myself, 'I think I remember seeing it happen, and I think I remember photographing it . . . but I'm not sure.' Because I was so frightened. I can remember the camera to my eye, but I was trying to remember whether the shutter was going off. It was such an intense thing.

"I was lucky. There were people killed on both sides of me. I don't know how I escaped without being hit . . . it's something I'll always be thankful for."

The girl in the photo, Mary Ann Vecchio, was not a student at Kent State. She turns out to be a fourteen-year-old runaway from Florida, just drifting through campus on this day.

Jeff Miller wasn't a radical or a leader, in fact, he was not politically active. He liked playing drums, wore his hair long, was shy of girls, and was concerned about social problems. He felt angered and betrayed by the Cambodian invasion.

The students' toll at Kent State stands at four dead and five badly wounded. Among the guardsmen, one man was injured on the arm by a rock.

1971 Feature
Hiding in Shadows

"It was a real shock to my senses . . . like nothing I had ever seen before. Warehouse people—many of them naked, with excrement smeared on their bodies. All kinds of weird sounds . . . horrible smells. It was just a total sensory confrontation."

Jack Dykinga, photographer for the *Chicago Sun-Times,* records life at the Lincoln and Dixon state schools for the retarded, in Illinois. "For the first hour and a half, I didn't take any pictures at all. I just watched . . . sort of overcome by the horror. Just the sheer terror of the whole thing."

Inside the crowded day rooms of these mammoth institutions, euphemistically called schools, thousands of retarded children and adults—society's discards—live an existence of utter degradation, loneliness, and despair. Hopelessness has worn away any remnant of pride and motivation. In these depersonalized warehouses, they are herded around like animals . . . robbed of any chance to progress and grow. The wandering specters, sedated with drugs, quietly languish away. The more aggressive ones are tied to chairs, until the staff can attend to them.

Grossly understaffed and overworked, the nurses and child-care aides are forced into assembly-line care. Aides feed, bathe, clothe, give medication, and maintain the overall social order. In one ward, or "cottage," there are four aides to care for 100 children; another unit of 112 is attended by one aide. There is no time for love and attention . . . only for custodial care. And even these basics are neglected—meals fed at ten times the normal rate, baths once a week, urine-soaked linen, bed sores, and malformed, curved limbs from lack of exercise.

An aide: "With enough help, we wouldn't have all this. These kids are human beings . . . they need care —oh, much more care. They can sense when they get more affection, and they can tell when people who are overworked get a little hostile toward them."

In the aftermath of the *Chicago Sun-Times* coverage, the state funding for the Department of Mental Health, previously scheduled to be cut, is reinstated at the same level.

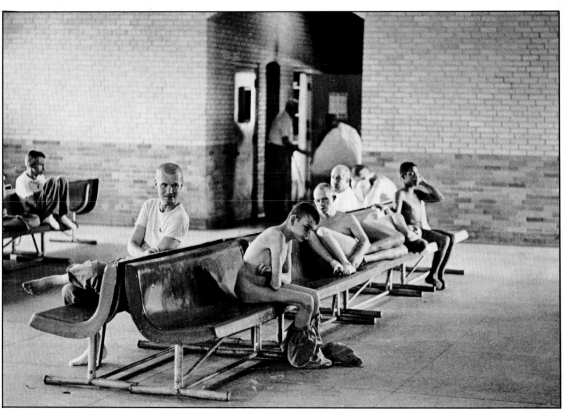

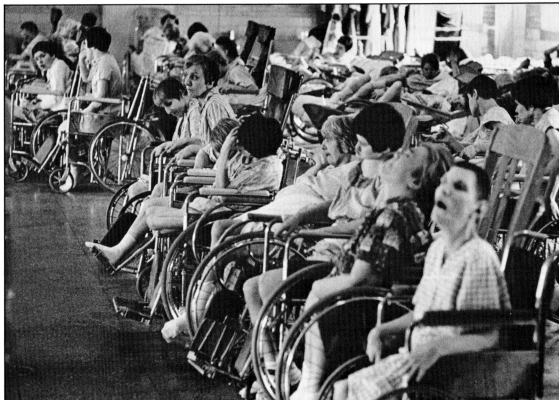

1972 Death in Dacca

The surgery performed on the Indian subcontinent, after the British-Indian conflict of 1947, leaves dangerous scars. Out of formerly Anglo-ruled India emerges a jigsaw puzzle—the country of Pakistan, divided into east and west, the 1,000-mile geographical gap between them filled by India. The two countries remain hostile neighbors, the festering hatred that stands between them stemming from deep-seated differences in religion and culture. Suppressed hostilities erupt to the surface in 1971—for the third time since partition.

Horst Faas, an eight-year veteran AP photographer of the Vietnam War and Pulitzer Prize winner of 1965, is covering the conflict from Calcutta, India. Michel Laurent, also an AP combat photographer, works out of Dacca in East Pakistan.

The latest Indo-Pakistani war grows out of the clash between the West Pakistani Punjabi culture and the Bengali culture of East Pakistan. Since early in the year, the movement for autonomy in East Pakistan has swelled.

March 26, 1971 . . . East Pakistan's first public declaration of independence as the new country of Bangladesh. West Pakistani President Mohammed Yahya Khan, in a frenzied effort to prevent secession, sanctions a wave of butchery against the rebellious eastern wing and imprisons Sheikh Mujibur Rahman, leader of the independence movement, for treason. After a series of battles, Yahya Khan's army emerges victorious. A reign of violence claims the lives of 1 million Bengalis and sends 10 million fleeing into India.

India, burdened with supporting the 10 million Bengali refugees who run from the Pak Army, plans for an East Pakistani reversal. A Bangladesh guerrilla force of 100,000, known as the Mukti Bahini, is secretly trained and equipped by India. With the alliance of the Indian Army and the Mukti Bahini forces, the Pak Army is forced to fight a two-front war. After thirteen days, Yahya Khan's troops surrender on December 17, 1971, ensuring the independence of Bangladesh.

Reprisals begin immediately in Bangladesh, even as joyous throngs celebrate. The Mukti Bahini are in no mood to take prisoners. They want vengeance. Suspected Pakistani collaborators and captured Pak soldiers are dragged into the streets for lynching amid cries of "Victory to Bangladesh."

On December 18 at Dacca Race Track . . . the first public

rally of Bangladesh. Photographer Laurent stays to cover the speakers, while Faas wanders through the crowd photographing faces. Along the way, Faas discovers this savage scene. Surrounded by a mass of 5,000 spectators, four prisoners, arms tied behind their backs, are being tortured by a small band of Mukti Bahini. For an hour the horror continues—clubbing, kicking, and cigarette burns . . . finally, the grisly bayonetting. The crowd jeers the prisoners mercilessly. Faas and Laurent are inside the circle of death, only steps away from the rifles thrusting with fixed bayonets.

"When the crowd closed in to stomp the victims, we pushed our way outside the nightmarish scene. I was bathed in sweat, even though it was a cool evening. My hands were trembling. Michel and I were too numbed to talk. He was pale, like the dying men. I probably was, too."

The photos of bayonetting are refused transmission, because they are "detrimental to the national interests." They eventually reach London in a disguised photo package. Faas and Laurent cover the story in concert and enter the photo series as a two-man team.

Michel Laurent is later killed in South Vietnam—April 28, 1975, the last newsman or photographer to die covering the thirty-year Indochina War.

1972 **Feature**
Scorched Earth

The effects of continuous warfare on Vietnam . . . little remains
but scorched earth. Napalm bombs and strafing attacks
have devastated the landscape. Chemical defoliation has
stripped the mountains of their abundant luxury woods—ebony,
teak, rosewood and mahogany. Entire crops are destroyed.

American ground troops are returning steadily to the States
as a result of Nixon's Vietnamization program of the early
seventies—the plan to shift major responsibility for ground
defense to the South Vietnamese. But United States
participation in the air war intensifies and spreads into Laos and
Cambodia, where B-52 bombers drop their load over the North
Vietnamese supply route, the Ho Chi Minh Trail. Intense
bombing of North Vietnam alternates with cease-fire
agreements in an effort to force negotiations. It seems like the
end is near, but the United States cannot seem to shake this
war. It just won't go away.

Covering the war for United Press International, Dave
Kennerly walks amid shattered trees and comes across this
American soldier cautiously approaching a Vietcong bunker.
Smoke billows from an air strike in the distant hills.

1973 The Day It Rained Fire

One small battle in a never-ending war.

June 8, 1972.

Trang Bang, twenty-five miles west of Saigon, is being held by North Vietnamese forces. The Vietcong have run a blockade across Route 1, which links Trang Bang to the capital. For three days, South Vietnamese foot soldiers press them, desperately trying to open up the highway. But the North is firmly entrenched.

The deadlock must be broken. The South Vietnamese Air Force is called in for support. They slice through the air, flying low over Route 1 toward Trang Bang. A small cluster of South Vietnamese—a few soldiers, women and children—gather along the road.

Something is wrong! The planes swoop down on the helpless group in dive runs that unleash their gruesome load. Napalmed . . . by their own people! A hideous accident that sends down more grief on these miserable souls who have seen nothing but war their whole lives. Today it rains fiery jelly.

Phan Thi Kim Phuc, having torn off her burning clothes, is running from the napalm area with the others. That is the only thing to do. Run and scream and cry. It is the same bone-chilling horror that tears their battered hearts time after time.

South Vietnamese combat photographer Huynh Cong "Nick" Ut is twenty-two years old and has grown up with the constant presence of war. He is traveling Route 1 on foot. This is how he covers the war, continually moving over the countryside. Up ahead, Ut sees the napalm and the frenzy. He records a moment so horrible the American people, dulled by an unending, remote war, are deeply moved. The war finally touches them.

Ut: "I'm a photographer in the field. Wherever the action is, I want to go." His older brother, also an AP combat photographer, was killed while on assignment in the delta region in 1965. Ut himself was wounded four months later a few feet from the scene of this picture—his fourth wound.

Meanwhile, the bombardiers—in quiet seclusion at 2,000 feet—continue their missions day by day, unaware of the trail of carnage they leave behind, the smell of burnt hair and flesh.

1973 Feature
The Moment of Life . . . an Experience Shared

The husband is pacing the floor in the hospital waiting room, chain-smoking cigarettes, his pocket full of cigars, reading the three-year-old sports magazine he finds among all the *House Beautiful* magazines and religious tracts . . . the woman is isolated in a sterile room, drugged, alone, or surrounded by strangers. This is the typical maternity scene.

Now, more and more, couples are seeking a fulfilling experience. Witnessing the drama of birth is one of the finest moments of life . . . when life itself begins for another human being. Lynda and Jerry Coburn choose to share that moment with each other.

"We really believe in this Lamaze method of childbirth, and we think it would be good if in some way we could let other people experience what natural childbirth is all about."

With this desire to share their experience, Lynda and Jerry allow Brian Lanker, photographer for the *Topeka Capital-Journal,* to be there during the labor and delivery of their baby.

Jerry is essential to the birth of their child. He sits next to Lynda, holding her hand, helping her to time the contractions, and reminding her to push down for delivery. He shares the frightening pain and amazing grace of a life he helped conceive. He sees his daughter born.

Brian: "When it came time for the child to be born, and we were going in, Lynda asked if *I* was ready! I got all dressed up in my gown and cap and shoes and mask, and I went in. I was just in awe, so excited, so taken by this whole thing that to this day I do not remember making the photographs that I took."

In 1973, the Pulitzer Prize awards juxtapose two primal human experiences. One of the Pulitzer photographs comes out of Vietnam, capturing in one shocking moment the horror of war. The other Pulitzer comes out of Middle America with beautiful images of the birth of a child. War and birth . . . the extremes in which we live.

Lynda: "One minute your stomach is so big and then in a second you have this hot, little, heavy, wet body on top of you . . . it's overwhelming."
Brian: "What a miraculous feat to create a child. Everybody takes it for granted. I mean right now there are children being born all over."

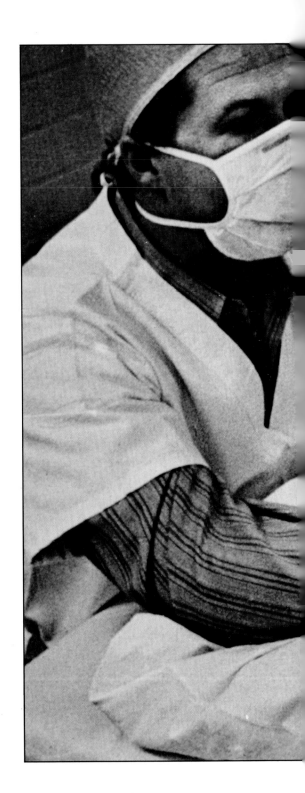

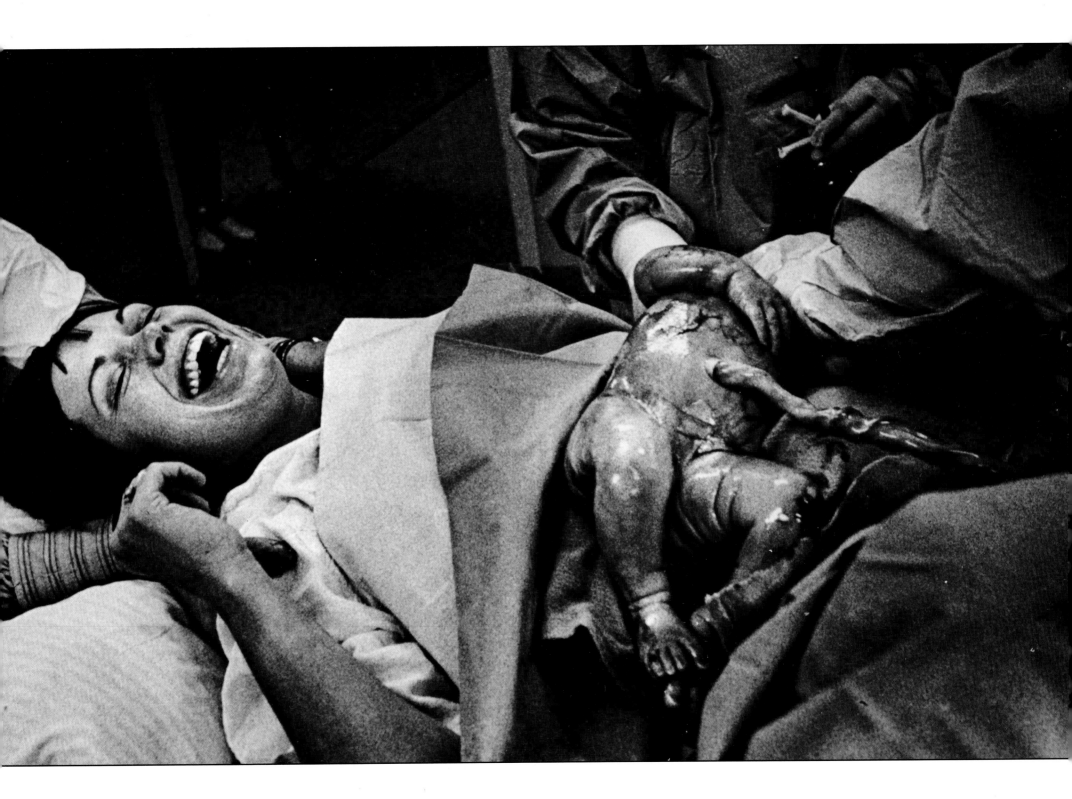

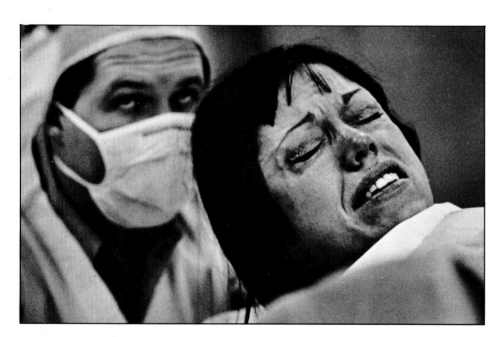

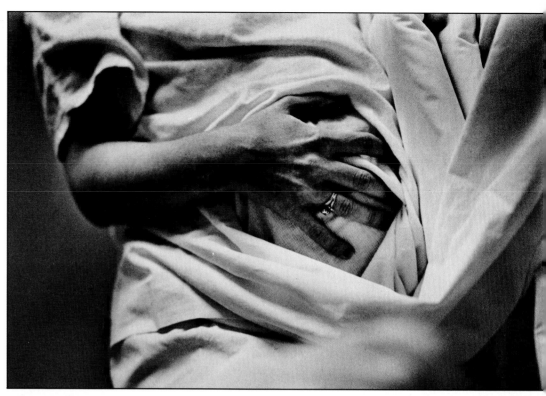

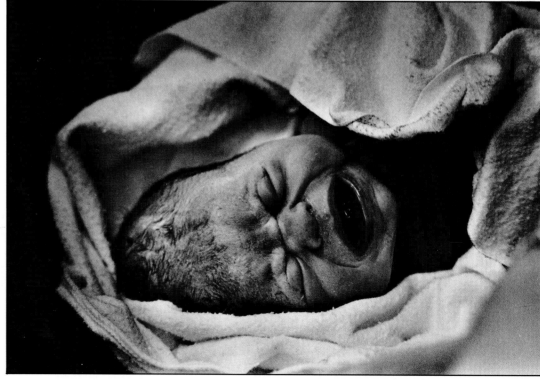

"I was excited beyond belief. I needed him to tell me what to do. It was the most important thing to me, having him there."

Jacki Lynn Coburn entered our world at 11:45 A.M., on Thursday, the 27th day of January, 1972.

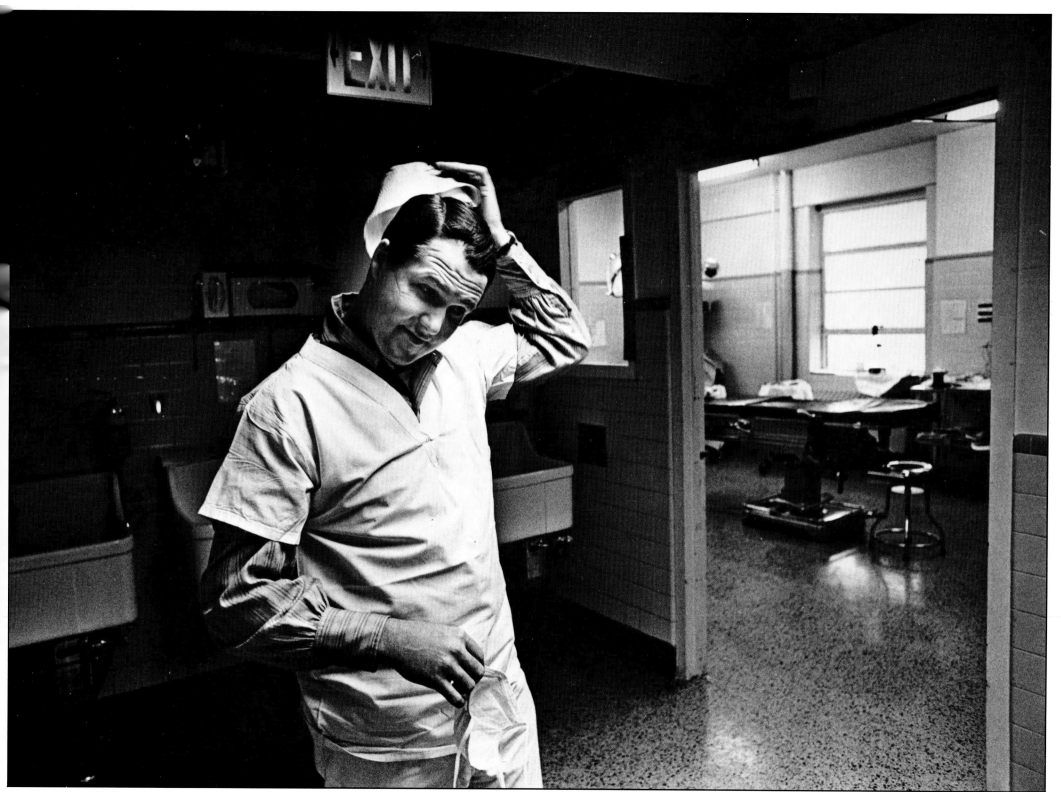

"I didn't think it would move me that much, but I was very surprised and excited inside."

1974 A Hollywood Drama

Anthony Roberts, a free-lance photographer, is pulling into the parking lot of a Hollywood discount store on a shopping errand. As he gets out of his car, he hears screams and shouting. Grabbing his camera, he runs across the lot and comes across a strange drama unfolding.

He sees a man holding a knife at the throat of a woman, while a security guard, George Derby, aims an automatic pistol at the attacker's head. The man, Ed Fisher, is attempting to kidnap Ellen Sheldon, wrestling her to the ground, as she comes out of the store.

As Derby corners them, he threatens to shoot Fisher if he does not drop the knife and release the woman. As Roberts records the tense drama, people pass by looking for the cameras . . . it seems as if a violent movie is being made.

Ellen struggles to her feet and Fisher grabs her, holding her tight. Again and again, George Derby demands that Fisher release the woman or he'll shoot. In his mind, George is not sure if he can shoot this man . . . but time is running out. The reasoning and the threats have not worked.

Suddenly, Fisher has the knife to her throat, and Derby reacts. He fires once, striking Fisher in the head, killing him instantly. He pulls back his gun.

Fisher lies dead on the asphalt. The drama lasted fifteen minutes . . . now it's over. Ellen Sheldon has knife slashes on her hand, but she is alive.

George Derby has done his job in the only way left open to him. He has just been forced to kill another human being, and he is in need of comfort. Unlike other Hollywood dramas, it's never easy.

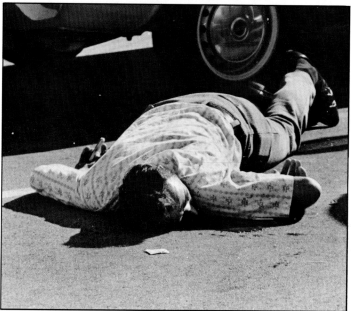

1974 Feature
Burst of Joy

For most people across America, this morning is like most others. But, for Lieutenant Colonel Robert Stirm, USAF, this morning is very special. He has dreamed for five years of this morning. He looks out the window of the plane as it touches down at Travis Air Force Base in California. It all seems the same. How could it be the same when he is so different?

Sal Veder, AP photographer, watches as the plane taxis to a stop. He is waiting for Bob, along with Bob's family . . . his wife, Loretta, Lori, 15, Robert, 14, Cynthia, 13, and Roger, 12.

Bob Stirm has spent more than five years in a North Vietnam prison camp. That's one thousand, eight hundred, and twenty-five mornings. . . away from his family. As he steps off the plane, he stands for a moment, facing his wife and children, who are running to greet him in a burst of joy. Then he goes forward.

For these men, the POWs of the Vietnam War, it can never be as it was. The years of separation and loneliness have taken their toll. Like many POW couples, Bob and Loretta are divorced in a year.

But his family had been strong in those five years. While he was caged, each day was a struggle to maintain his sense of self-worth. One of the things that keeps a man alive and sane is the unwavering knowledge that his family misses him.

This picture expresses beautifully how Robert Stirm made it back.

1975 Lull in the Battle

16529 Maplewild Avenue, SW . . .

John Neuffer and his family live in a modest two-story waterfront home in Burien, a small suburb south of Seattle. At 3:00 A.M., they are awakened from a sound sleep by their barking dog. Only a few days before, they had taken in the wandering mongrel; it had looked so lost and hungry, the children wanted to keep it.

Suddenly, they understand what the dog is warning them of . . . the house is on fire! John and his wife and two children have just enough time to escape the burning home before it explodes into flame.

When the firemen from King County get to the scene, the house is an inferno. They go to work. The house is on a very steep bank, and the hoses have to be run up and down the slippery hillside. It is hot and dangerous work. The exhausted men race through the mud and smoke in the dark predawn. They are losing the race. This time the fire will have its way. The house cannot be saved.

Jerry Gay, staff photographer for the *Seattle Times,* comes to work early in the morning and is sent to cover the story. By the time he gets to the scene, the house has burned down, but the firemen are still hard at work. Jerry is amazed by the courage and dedication of the firemen. "After more than five hours of fire fighting, most of the men were still there, cleaning up the wreckage. They were knocking down walls for safety. A heavy pall of smoke hung over everything."

Jerry climbs the steep bank and sees four firemen resting before going back to work. Grimy and sodden, they sit silently in the smoky dawn. They have done their best. Jerry takes their picture, recording a moment of authentic Americana. It could be a Norman Rockwell painting, speaking simply of honest hard work. After Vietnam, Watergate, and the uncertainty that came with the seventies, it is an eloquent restatement of American values.

1975 Feature
The Seventies . . . How Do You Like It So Far?

The Washington life-style has made a lot of great ink these last few years and photographer Matt Lewis, of the *Washington Post*'s Sunday magazine, *Potomac,* has been on it. Catching the many sides of Washington . . . from boxing to the status strut, Bella Abzug to Mean John Wilson, tough bosses to classy French restaurants. The pulse of the seventies in a great city . . . sports, politics, the high life, the mean streets, the people.

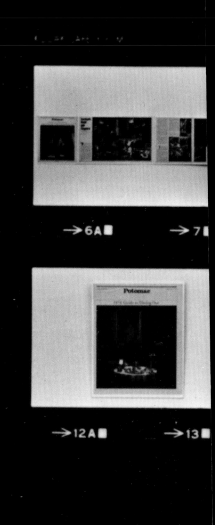

→6A ■   →7 ■

→12A ■   →13 ■

David Brinkley's Journey

The man behind the electronic mask

David Brinkley. News, comedy, news, and it's done.

THE PHANTOM IN THE LIMELIGHT

City Councilman Tedson Meyers on Neighborhoods and The City

Quotations from Attorney General Saxbe

How's that again?

By John Twohey

"They don't say... I'm not smart."

By George Lardner Jr.

1976 Two More Seconds

When the fire call comes across Boston's *Herald-American* city desk, photographer Stan Forman knows something unusual is going down. "The fire dispatcher was saying something about people trapped." He races to his car.

When he is four blocks from the burning apartment on Marlborough Street, he can see black smoke. He hears an SOS, from the fire chief on his radio, ordering a ladder truck to the rear of the building. Forman pulls over and starts running.

He sprints into the alley behind the building. "I was looking up as I ran, and I could see a fire fighter lowering himself from the room to a fire escape where a young woman and child were clinging. I knew in seconds they would all be together on the fire escape. In the alley, an engine company was laying hose, and Ladder Truck Thirteen pulled into place for a ladder rescue.

"I climbed onto the bed of the ladder truck to get pictures of the rescue. That put me about ten feet above the ground and that much closer to the fire escape where the fireman had just joined the woman and the child. Then the fire fighter's hand went up to grab the aerial ladder as it was being lowered, and suddenly someone screamed . . . or maybe it was the shriek of the metal as the fire escape balcony gave way. I watched everything give way through my lens, everyone falling.

"I remember thinking, I don't want to see them hit. I turned away before it would happen. I must have stood with my back to what was happening there on the ground for close to a minute. People were screaming. I was shaking. I didn't want to look.

"I still thought all three had gone down. Then I looked up, and there was the fire fighter still dangling from the ladder. I looked down. The woman and child fell behind a wooden fence into a little back yard. I saw the men coming out of the yard with the woman's body. The fire fighter who was trying to save them, a man named O'Neil, kept repeating, 'Two more seconds; two more seconds.'"

The child, Tiare Jones, lives and recovers. The woman, Diana Bryant, dies, her body breaking the child's fall. Stan Forman's photographs are circulated around the world. An outraged public demands tougher regulations and enforcement. Due to the inspection and repair of the fire equipment, a great many lives are saved.

Feature
Honk If You Oppose Busing

The 1975 school term in Louisville, Kentucky, approaches with uncertainty and fear growing day by day. The federal court order issued in July mandates busing, to achieve racial integration, in time for the opening of the school session on September 4. For the remainder of the summer, everyone knows busing is on its way, but many cannot believe that it will really happen here . . . now. It seems so drastic, so sudden.

Late summer. There are those who accept the busing order and plan for it—the school superintendent, the school board, the staff, the teachers, the police department. How to move 130,000 students? It involves a large-scale game of chess on redistricting maps, orientation meetings in new neighborhoods and new schools, special visitation programs to ease the change.

For a great many residents of Louisville and Jefferson counties, busing was, is, and forever shall be, wrong. Protests are held through the city—banners and signs: "Honk if you oppose busing." Placards invoke God and America's Founding Fathers as opponents of busing. The Concerned Parents Against Busing gain political sophistication, pouring on the pressure in this, an election year.

The big yellow buses rumble through the early morning mist carrying a mixed load of kids and state police. The abstract becomes concrete . . . 577 buses moving 90,000 kids. Ironically, this first day of school has been eased by the school boycott which keeps 40 percent of the students away. In the morning light, two classmates shake hands, making their tentative peace.

Hot nights and violence . . . clubs, sticks, and shouts . . . police in riot gear endure punishment and abuse . . . Confederate flags . . . fire bombings. The Ku Klux Klan takes advantage of the issue to further its own recruiting drive. Louisville sees two days of anti-busing fever raging out of control, with a chain of fires and vandalized businesses. After the tear gas clears, 100 people are found injured, and 200 are arrested.

The news staff: "Busing for racial integration happened in Louisville because a group of black parents backed by the NAACP started the wheels of the federal courts turning in a lawsuit. Central to the litigation was the idea that black children were being deprived of an equal education, without the chance to associate with white children. Busing has brought black and white together. Louisville, touched to its core, is a different place for its experience."

The entire twenty-seven-member photographic staff of the *Courier-Journal* and the *Louisville Times* contributes to the seventy-picture portfolio, a graphic description of the effect of busing issue on Louisville and Jefferson counties, from August to December of 1975. Through foresight, they are able to avoid media-provoked incidents and publicity-seeking, and present instead well-rounded coverage that is representative of what is really happening in the schools and on the streets.

1977 Right Wing–Left Wing

In 1973, as our involvement in Vietnam wears down, rioting left-wing students overthrow Thailand's pro-American rightist dictator, Thanom Kittikachorn. A neutralist government is formed, which immediately requests that the 50,000 American soldiers and the squadrons of bombers be withdrawn.

By 1976, Thailand's powerful conservative forces, fearful of the country's drift to the left and the influence of her Communist neighbors, plan a coup. The showdown between Thailand's left wing and right wing has come.

In September, ex-dictator Thanom returns from exile on a visit. When the leftist demand for his expulsion is not met, 4,000 students take over Thammasat University, bringing in guns and grenades. A few days later, while putting up anti-Thanom posters, two students are seized by police and lynched.

The students occupying the university retaliate by staging a mock hanging, lynching an effigy of Crown Prince Vajiralongkorn. The newspapers splash the pictures on page one. Enraged by the insult to the monarchy, 10,000 rightist students gather outside the gates of the university. Now the time has come—1,500 Special Warfare Police move in. Armed with automatic weapons and bazookas, they batter down the barricaded gates and blast their way into the crowds, followed by the gleeful rightists.

It is a calculated and savage four-hour bloodbath. Many leftists are shot or beaten to death. Those trying to escape hurl themselves into the river, but many are captured by the mob . . . one student is beheaded, another's eyes are gouged out, eight are lynched. The lifeless bodies are still beaten and mutilated. Then the bodies are piled up, doused with gasoline, and burned.

At the end, hundreds of boys and girls are stripped and methodically beaten. After four hours, 39 students are dead, 180 maimed. AP photographer Neal Ulevich, whose photographs record the atrocity, has grim memories of the day. "If there is any value in the pictures, it is that they may have made some people pause and think about wider issues, such as hatred and violence."

Their fury still not spent, the 10,000 rightists, cheered on by spectators, move on to the Government House and demand the resignation of the Prime Minister . . . and get it. Thailand's fourteenth postwar coup is over. From this shockingly bloody riot, a military junta rises to power. Strongly anti-Communist and pro-American, they veer to the right.

The new strongmen promise to restore democracy . . . and then proclaim martial law, suspend the constitution, and censor the press. Meanwhile, the Communists step up their activity in the northeast provinces.

1977 The Soiling of Old Glory

1976 . . . America's Bicentennial year here in her cradle of Liberty—Boston. Everywhere, flags are flying patriotically. Except for one. Here the Stars and Stripes has been transformed into a weapon of hatred. This kind of raw, ugly racism hides behind increasingly sophisticated masks. This time the issue is busing in South Boston.

Two hundred white students gather outside Boston City Hall, carrying signs and banners . . . chanting anti-busing slogans. They sweep into City Hall in an attempt to force a list of demands on City Council, but find only empty chambers.

A moment of group inspiration, as they recite: "I pledge allegiance to the flag . . . with liberty and justice for all."

Suddenly, a group of twenty splinters off from the main bunch, erupting in violence. "Get the nigger; kill him."

Stanley Forman of the *Boston Herald-American* is out cruising when his police radio alerts him to "trouble on City Hall Plaza." He arrives just ahead of the police and sees Theodore Landsmark, a black lawyer, walking briskly toward City Hall, unaware of the imminent danger. "Suddenly, they were all over him—punching, whacking, knocking him to the ground. Through my lens I observed the flagstaff, the flag furled about it, its pinnacle being thrust at the head of the helpless black man. He struggled up from the pavement, with his attackers restraining him as they would steady a target for the benefit of a marksman."

Theodore Landsmark is treated at the hospital for a broken nose, facial cuts, and bruises over most of his body.

It's not a proud day for Old Glory.

1977 Feature
Dedicated to Eddie Robinson

It is raining the day that Chattanooga holds her Armed Forces Day Parade. Robin Hood, photographer for the *Chattanooga News-Free Press,* moves through the crowd along the road, looking for the meaning.

"I felt the real story was not in the pomp and ceremony of the parade, but in the emotions of the spectators viewing it."

Far from the reviewing stand, filled with dignitaries and honored guests, sits a veteran who lost both legs in the Vietnam War. His name is Eddie Robinson. As the sounds of the parade swirl about, he clutches his small child closely to him. He is rain-drenched, wearing an army poncho, an old army shirt and hat.

"Here was a man who had made a great sacrifice, lost in the crowd, biting his lip. I had, seconds before, finished photographing a Vietnam refugee, his wife, and three children waving American flags . . . not fifty feet away. Here was this guy, lost in the crowd, who paid a high price for their freedom . . . and ours."

Like Eddie Robinson, a wounded America goes on, with courage and hope.

1978 Live on TV . . . A National Hero

When Richard Hall gets to work Tuesday morning, Anthony Kiritsis is waiting for him. Pulling a gun on him as Hall walks into the office, Kiritsis wraps one end of a wire around Hall's neck and ties the other end to the barrel of a .12 gauge sawed-off shotgun. That holds the shotgun tight against the back of Hall's head. Then Kiritsis wires the trigger of the shotgun directly to his own neck, so that if a sharpshooter tries to pick him off, the shotgun would automatically blow Hall's head off as Kiritsis goes down. Now Anthony Kiritsis is ready to take his revenge.

Hall is the president of the Meridian Mortgage Company, a brokerage firm that lent Kiritsis money to build a shopping center. But Kiritsis claims the mortgage company didn't back him, and in fact discouraged potential lessors in order to force him into bankruptcy, and a foreclosure for their own profit. Having already invested his life savings, and with the loan due in a matter of days, he feels that he's been swindled and he holds Hall responsible.

Kiritsis pushes Hall out of the building and down the sidewalk, cautioning the gathering crowd to stand clear. Terrified, Hall walks stiffly, like a sleepwalker. They are a strange sight on a Tuesday morning in Indianapolis. Seeing them, a patrolling police car stops in the street near them to investigate. Kiritsis, threatening to take Hall's life, commandeers the car and forces Hall to drive them back to his apartment.

Within hours, the quiet suburban apartment complex is an armed fortress. There are more than 200 officers on the scene . . . state police, sheriff's department, city police, and a S.W.A.T. team. When Kiritsis warns them that he has wired the windows of his apartment with dynamite, the police evacuate the building.

Driving in his car on the way to Indianapolis, freelance photographer John Blair listens to the truckers talking on the CB about Kiritsis. It is Wednesday afternoon. Blair had gotten a phone call that morning from UPI with orders to rush down to help in the round-the-clock coverage of the situation, already in its second day. "I don't blame him," he hears one trucker say. The trucker on the other end agrees. "I hope he gets what he's going after, as long as he doesn't kill the guy."

More and more people come forward with allegations of fraud against the mortgage company. Anthony Kiritsis has captured the imagination of all the people who feel ripped off and frustrated by the financial institutions that control their lives. He is becoming a folk hero.

By the time John Blair gets to the scene, the media has completely engulfed the apartment complex . . . more than a hundred reporters and photographers from all over the country—wire services, radio, and network news teams. It has become an "event." Like David against Goliath, Anthony Kiritsis has taken them all on . . . the mortgage company, the cops, the media, the whole system. People are identifying with his anger; it looks right somehow.

The people who live in the apartments are mostly older folks, and they accept the siege in good spirits, offering their hospitality to the hordes of police and newspeople. Elderly ladies feed cookies to hungry cops; tired reporters sleep on apartment floors. UPI rents an apartment from an occupant, a sort of three-day sublease, that is used by John Blair and the other photographers as their headquarters. For the next 24 hours, they wait while the negotiators try to strike a deal with Kiritsis. With everyone milling around the complex, the mood becomes almost festive.

By Thursday, the third day, they have negotiated his demands. He is promised immunity by the prosecutor's office and a news conference to tell his side of the story. But Blair sees the snipers taking position outside Kiritsis' door. It is a ruse. If Kiritsis comes out armed, but without Hall, they are going to kill him.

There is an ominous, tense silence as Kiritsis finally steps out of his apartment. They are still wired together. Hall grasps the wire around his neck, desperately trying to keep the shotgun from being triggered. In a stiff, measured walk they come down the stairs and across the street to another building. Blair has positioned himself in the lobby for the expected news conference, but no one knows for sure where or how it is going to happen. Suddenly Kiritsis stops, so close to Blair that the photographer could reach out and touch the shotgun. Kiritsis whirls around to the camera team. "Get those goddamn television cameras rolling, I want everyone to hear what I have to say!''

This is the first time that anyone has gotten a good look at Kiritsis since it all began. Pointing at Hall, he screams at him in a rage as he tells his garbled story. He tries to make Hall read a statement accepting fault for the whole incident, forgiving Kiritsis for what he has done, and making the loan of $130,000 ''no longer due and payable.''

Hall, exhausted and emotionally drained, can only stammer. Kiritsis, near the breaking point, begins to cry. At that moment, it becomes obvious to Blair that anything could happen. ''I had a gut feeling in that moment that Kiritsis would blow Hall away, or turn the gun on himself.'' The emotional energy in the room saturates everyone. Blair, who is standing in front of Hall and in point-blank range of the shotgun, moves aside. Hall's eyes are closed in shock, or in prayer. John Blair senses the moment and takes the picture.

Three microphones are poking into this stilled moment . . . the whole scene is being carried live on network TV. People sitting at home in their living rooms see it as it is happening, in that deadly hallway, as if they were there in that same space and time. Suddenly it is real to them. The cold scrutiny of the TV camera reveals his wild eyes. They see that Kiritsis isn't a hero at all. He's crazy.

''I'm a goddamn national hero, and don't you forget it!'' Kiritsis screams. Adding to this bizarre scene, one network station in Indianapolis cuts off the live drama, leaving a blank screen for a few moments, because Kiritsis is using ''bad language.''

The ''press conference'' ends as suddenly as it began. Kiritsis leads Hall through the lobby area and into an open apartment. The S.W.A.T. team immediately clears the lobby and runs outside to cover the building. The newspeople and the photographers wait outside in the street.

Then they hear the shotgun blast. ''You can't imagine what feelings went through everyone at that moment. We all thought, 'Oh, God, it's happened.' ''

Actually, inside the apartment, Kiritsis releases Hall as soon as they get inside and safely away from the snipers that he

knows are all around. Then Kiritsis goes to the patio of the apartment and fires his shotgun into the air. He wants everyone to know—the cops, the media, Hall himself, and the viewers on TV—that he wasn't fooling around. Then Kiritsis walks out and gives himself up.

Richard Hall is sent to the hospital for observation and shock. Anthony Kiritsis is found not guilty of kidnapping by reason of insanity and placed in a mental hospital.

What would have happened to other popular folk heroes, like Bonnie and Clyde, or Billy the Kid, if they had been seen live on TV as they committed their crimes . . . instead of people hearing about it in legend afterward?

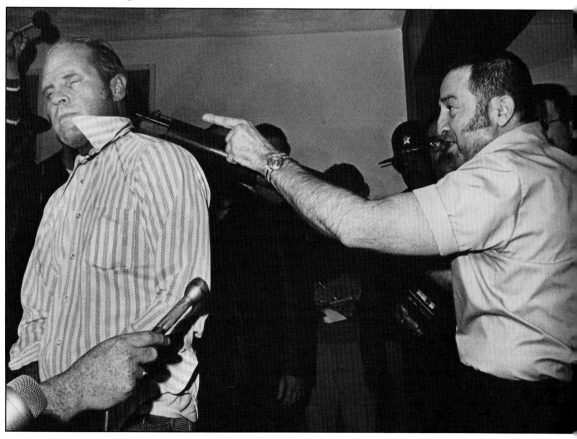

Feature
The Outlaw Nation

For most of Salisbury, the capital of Rhodesia, it is a time for garden parties and weekend barbeques in the soft, welcoming air of a new summer. It is a good life for the fair-skinned in the clear, limitless horizon that defines southern Africa.

But it is increasingly difficult to maintain this air of easy resplendence. The races have existed in mutual fear and tension over the years, a legacy from the British colonial era. The official government policy of racial segregation mandates two very separate bodies of law regarding voting privileges, public education, housing, health care, and land ownership. This vise grip of restrictive legislation maintains white supremacy on the canvas of a nation whose dominant color is ebony. The color wheel of Rhodesia: ninety-four parts black, four parts white, two parts Asian.

White-ruled Rhodesia has pressed on in spite of worldwide boycotts and United Nations sanctions, becoming in the eyes of the world, an outlaw nation. In an effort to gain a power base for a new representational government, guerrillas appear throughout the countryside, their numbers growing enormously from the mid-sixties through the seventies. These two divergent visions of the future of Rhodesian life come at each other in a violent clash of wills, spreading into all-out civil war.

Alone in the pre-dawn darkness, AP photographer J. Ross Baughman waits in the center square of Salisbury for his lift to the front lines. Finally, out of the stillness, an army truck makes its way down the road and rumbles to a halt in front of him. The truck is filled with Grey Scout cavalry, uniformed and geared for a military mission. Baughman climbs aboard, loaded down with gear of a different sort . . . several camera bodies, lenses, and a case full of film. He is immediately handed a weapon and the camouflage fatigues of the Scouts as a prerequisite for going along. The truck breaks its idle, bucking and lurching ahead into the tribal hinterlands of black Rhodesia, into the heart of guerrilla-held territory.

The screeching of brakes alerts the men to their arrival at base camp; they shake free the hours of travel weariness. The Grey Scouts, an actual fighting cavalry renowned for its tracking abilities, are preparing for a series of search-and-destroy strikes among the black villages near the Botswana

border. Their job is to hunt down resisters to the white minority government and its policy of official racism.

For Ross Baughman, it has been an uphill battle to get this far. The press corps in Salisbury is restricted from the war zone except for brief, official morning-after tours. Baughman's goal was to finesse his way past this red tape and see actual combat action. He asked to go out with the Grey Scouts twice but had been turned down both times.

While mingling at one of the monthly Saturday afternoon barbeques given for American mercenaries, Baughman meets the field commander of the Scouts who also happens to be the highest-ranking American in the Rhodesian army. A man who likes to maintain a high profile, the Field Commander smells the opportunity for some newsprint—the kind of wide coverage Baughman's wire story and pictures could provide for the folks back home. Two short questions later—"Can you ride? Can you shoot?"—and he was taking responsibility for pushing through Baughman's clearance papers to the Greys' base camp.

"I was anxious to see more of the ground effort, the really exhausting ground fighting that was going on, and I was anxious to find more Americans who were fighting in the Rhodesian army. We all knew they were there. In almost every unit you'd find at least one. These guys thought of themselves as ideological mercenaries; they felt they were fighting against Communism and so they just wanted to go wherever the latest conflict was. They were mostly Vietnam veterans who wanted to keep on fighting.

". . . I was coming along as the newcomer, just trying my best to get into the field and take real pictures and get a firsthand story. I couldn't stand just accepting the government's press releases."

The mission . . . to "neutralize the area." Cavalry men who had been dispersed all over Rhodesia are brought together and introduced to one limited sector near Wencke National Park. Each troop carries out a systematic interrogation of all villages in their district with orders to search for guerrilla sympathizers, money, and caches of weapons. It is potentially fertile ground; white men haven't been here for years.

"What the Grey Scouts would typically do is begin from the

scene of a guerrilla raid, maybe they'd robbed a store or held up a bus. These guys would figure out whose footprints were whose and then go off in a logical direction. But the guerrillas would usually stick together for only a mile or two or three and then go in all different directions. So the Scouts would have to pick out one set and eventually follow those tracks to a village.

"They show up at a village. The squad leader can usually speak the language, so he'll begin questioning them, calmly at first, to try and see if they're cooperating. But if they felt they were getting too much of an act, then they might try either psychological pressure or actual physical abuse.

"On my troop's mission, they forced all the men in one

village to line up in push-up stance on the ground. It was very hot that day, upper nineties. They're holding that position for forty-five minutes in the sun, many of them starting to shake violently from muscle fatigue. As their knees would bend or their backs collapse in, the soldiers would give them a swift kick. They said that the first guy who fell would be taken away. And eventually, the first guy fell. They took him around the back of the building, knocked him out, and fired a shot in the air. They continued bringing men to the back of the building. The poor guy on the end was crying and going crazy, and he finally broke and started talking. As it turns out, what he was saying wasn't true, but the Scouts were willing to use it as a lead."

During the stake-out at another village, the soldiers discover that the village's ranking authority, a sort of mayor, has his name on the roster of a legal black nationalist party. The Scouts believe that because he is a local politician who supports black nationalism and independence, he knows the whereabouts of the guerrillas. Baughman watches as the lieutenant tries to get answers out of the man by beating his head with a bat, stopping only when he lay unconscious, his jaw broken. Later he is revived and savagely tortured, along with his wife and daughter. Before leaving, they destroy three granaries which provide the village's sustenance for the entire upcoming dry season, forcing the villagers at gunpoint to ruin the grain by spreading it over the dirt.

Most of Ross Baughman's film documenting his two weeks with the Grey Scouts is confiscated by censors and shredded. But anticipating this, Baughman has hidden three rolls of film in a secret pocket in his camera bag, which he succeeds in smuggling out of the country.

"With these photographs I mean to humanize the facts and figures of a war story. I want to show the experience and the intensity that people go through so that next time you read '12 Killed in Rhodesian Conflict,' you'll understand how ugly a person-to-person war it really is."

In 1980, the civil war ends with a black nationalist victory. Robert Mugabe, a guerrilla leader, is elected Prime Minister. After clinging fiercely to an era long out of time and out of place with modern Africa, Rhodesia joins the fold as the new black nation of Zimbabwe.

1979 In the Quiet Beyond Town

They all live together in the large colonial house, just one big happy family. A country place set out in the quiet beyond town. The family settled in this spot outside the small Pennsylvania town many years before. Richard Greist and his brother, Joseph, grew up here; each has married and are raising their children together in this same house.

There had been tragedy in the house before today. Ten years ago, there was a fire and their mother had burned to death. But they had rebuilt and gone on, and in time, the smell of smoke faded away, but was not forgotten.

Richard works as an aide in a mental hospital. He comes home for lunch, as usual, and is last seen walking up the driveway with his pregnant wife Janice, arm in arm, talking and smiling. The neighbors all say he is "a nice guy, you know, just like you or me."

Tom Kelly, photographer for the *Pottstown Mercury,* is on the road, also headed for lunch, when he hears coming through the crackle of his police radio the dispatcher's call: "Attention, all cars respond . . . use extreme caution . . . suspect may be heavily armed." It continues: "Someone stabbing everybody . . . a woman lying on a front lawn, covered with blood . . . assist State Police and two ambulances."

Kelly wheels in just ahead of the incoming police cars which string out in a continually growing barracade along the road in front of the house. Greist's seventy-one-year-old grandmother is lying on the grass, stabbed in the face and neck, and is hastily attended to by ambulance paramedics.

Darting between police cars to get a good angle, Kelly crawls to within fifty feet of the house. There have been rumors of weapons inside, but as yet, there have been no shots. Fifty cops and newspeople, crouched behind a wall of cars, watch for a move or a sign. But there is nothing; only their own rustlings as they shift in place.

Joe Greist makes an urgent attempt to open up a line of communication to his brother, Richard, inside. His voice, amplified by a bullhorn, pleads with his brother to come out. But, there is no answer.

The first hour is a standoff. No one knows what is happening in the house. But they know this: Earlier, Joe had rushed the front door and managed to rescue two children, his own child and one of his brother's. Fortunately, Joe's second child is at school for the day. That leaves Beth Ann, Richard's other child, and Richard's wife still trapped inside.

Suddenly, the front door opens. Little Beth Ann walks out. She is covered with blood. She has been stabbed in the face and eyes many times with a screwdriver. She walks very slowly, unable to see, toward the line of police and Tom Kelly. Then she looks up at them, blood streaming from both eyes, and says, "Please don't hurt my daddy."

"What I saw was horrible. I couldn't raise my camera to take a picture. The camera did not come up. With eight years working on the street, I thought I had seen everything until I saw her."

A cop breaks from cover, a shotgun in his hand, and scoops her up. Kelly reacts by raising his camera and photographing Officer Doug Weaver's smile of relief . . . at least she was alive. Kelly cannot see the image clearly; he is crying.

As Beth Ann is rushed off in an ambulance, Joseph once again pleads with his brother to surrender. There is just uneasy silence as each precious minute is lost. Not knowing what Richard Greist has done or might do to his pregnant wife, the police realize they must storm the door.

When they get through the front door, they find him standing there, his bare chest smeared with blood. They grab him and he cries, "Hold me, I'm afraid." They start down the front walk toward custody, but in the confusion of the moment, Greist breaks free and charges directly forward, straight for Kelly, screaming, "I didn't do it; Joe did it." Only four feet away, Kelly snaps the single frame of Greist, streaked with blood, running wildly from the house. Moments later, he is wrestled to the ground and handcuffed.

Inside the house, Janice Greist and her unborn child are found stabbed to death and mutilated. Even the family cat has been cut to shreds.

Kelly: "Later, Greist said that he had spent the night before in a churchyard, and he had seen demons all around him. He said he saw the Devil in his little girl's eyes."

Ruled insane, the murder charges against Richard Greist are dropped. Now in a mental hospital, his appeal for release is being considered.

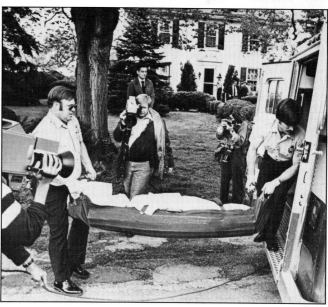

On Sunday evening, February 5, as New Englanders wind down from their weekend by taking in the news on TV, they hear the National Weather Service predict a new round in their continuing bout with winter . . . a six-inch snowfall. Barely enough to catch the attention of Bostonians this season. Only two weeks ago, they had shoveled out of twenty-one inches.

The snow begins falling Monday morning about 8:30. Most of the school kids and work force have already set out for the day. Some swear there is a strangeness to how it begins, a kind of ominous hiss as the snow hits ground. By early afternoon, no one has any doubts about the storm's determination. Schools and office buildings begin to empty out early as people scatter for home.

The weathermen revise and re-revise, now looking for eight to fourteen inches. Snow removal equipment combs the major commuter routes, trying to eat away enough of the stuff to create traffic lanes. As tractor-trailers jackknife and cars careen on the roads of eastern Massachusetts, all chance for a reprieve vanishes. It will be a treacherous rush-hour run.

The weather satellite crew sends out a warning . . . "Do not venture out unless absolutely necessary." With Connecticut and Rhode Island already battered to a halt, Massachusetts braces for a full-scale state of emergency. By late afternoon, the snow is being whipped up by frightening hurricane-force winds reaching 120 mph, roaring like a freight train across the buried land.

A wall of white clogs the night air as it delivers its load, leaving drifts that measure more than eight feet. Commuters frantically search for their cars among a whole line of indistinguishable mounds of snow. After digging out, they head for the few open arteries. Straining to see, they spend the evening inching along, hoping to clear each familiar spot along the way—the next bend, the distant mileage marker, the upcoming exit. Hope runs out for the 3,000 drivers left stranded on Route 128, the major beltway around Boston. They are suddenly like aliens in unfamiliar territory, miles from warmth and safety, trapped in a hostile environment that makes a mockery of the suits and ties, the high heels and nylons of their indoor world. They are trapped.

Chief photographer Kevin Cole of the *Boston Herald*

American: "That line of cars went on for miles around that bend. They had nowhere to go. Emergency equipment couldn't get anywhere. Everything just stopped. It was everybody for themselves and some people died in those cars waiting for help."

Cole is off work for the day, at home in the coastal town of Plymouth. "I had never seen anything like it and I've lived on the water all my life. The waves were mammoth. They would take the chunk of land you were standing on and pull it right out. I started taking pictures down at a restaurant on the water where the waves were coming right over the top of the roof. It was warm, I can remember, because I was in the water up to my waist. Then, all of a sudden, it turned cold. It was almost an instant thing. It just turned freezing cold. Things started to ice by the time I got home. Then the snow started. It was unbelievable. The next morning when I woke, the entire house was buried; you couldn't see out the windows."

Thousands are stranded all along the coast. The sea ignores all proprieties, crashing through perimeters of long-established sea walls. Voracious tidewaters rip away what the beach dwellers had thought was their own, biting off chunks of the granite sea walls and beach . . . followed by roofing, floorboard, and dreams. Driven by howling winds, the surf gnaws here and there at land, reshaping the entire coastline. Thirty-foot swells sink seven ships. A pilot boat that goes to the aid of an oil tanker taking on water in Salem Sound is lost at sea, with all hands aboard.

As the water and ice floes take over coastal towns, terrified residents climb onto roofs and second-floor porches to escape their flooded homes. Clinging to roof gutters for support, they can only wait and pray for the police and fire department rescue boats, the "ducks," to bring them to shelter centers—in high schools, armories, even movie theaters. Splintered houses are strewn along the beach, lying at odd angles to each other, or upside down, looking like matchboxes or wooden blocks abandoned in child's play. Some homes float out to sea.

Declared a disaster area by Governor Dukakis and President Carter, Army and National Guard troops arrive by the thousands on giant military transports, along with tons of heavy equipment and emergency resources, turning greater Boston into an armed camp. They airlift desperately needed food to refugees in relief shelters and take on the massive snow clearing operation with their scoop loaders, backhoes, and bulldozers. Doctors and nurses hitch rides to hospitals on jeeps and Army trucks. Police in riot gear keep watch over continual outbreaks of lawlessness; more than 125 looters are arrested.

Holding two days worth of film on the coastal disaster, Cole is resolved to get it into town and on the presses. His plan is to make his way over to Hyannis Airport on Cape Cod and catch a small plane into Boston. The local service station owner offers Cole the use of his truck but flatly refuses his services as Cole's driver. Once out on the road, there is no life in sight . . . it looks like Antarctica. Finally connecting with the main drag to the Cape, he sees that the major state highway has been reduced to little more than a toboggan run. After a harrowing drive negotiating the slender white tunnel, the truck bouncing and rebounding from side to side, Cole finds the Hyannis Airport as battened down as Plymouth was.

A sign tempts him from across the way . . . Discover Flying School. Once inside, Cole makes a surprising discovery of his own. He finds the owner quite willing to introduce him to the pleasures of his open-air, two-seater, single-prop trainer plane. "I asked him if the thing could really fly. It looked like it ran on a wound-up rubber band." Airborne after a tortuously slow and bumpy climb, they tour up the coast, the pilot dipping the plane sideways while Cole takes pictures, returning to land with aerial film of the devastation.

Staff photographer Paul Benoit is determined to cover the besieged coastal town of Revere, where "ducks" ultimately rescue over a thousand people. There is a driving ban in effect in Boston and the metropolitan police have already nixed Benoit's request for a lift. There is only one way to get there . . . walk. "They told me I would never make it." He endures a grueling ten-hour trek, alone and on foot, through a blinding storm and a rising flood of water. After drying his camera in an oven, he goes straight to that part of town hardest hit, working three days and nights without sleep.

Getting in-progress coverage of the blizzard is only part of the work. The *Herald American* building is blacked out along with one-third of Boston, much of which spends twenty-four to

thirty-six hours without heat and light. Some of the staff members have been camped out here since the beginning. Photographer Leo Tierney has been holding down the fort at the *Herald*, processing any film that makes it into town by whatever methods can be jerryrigged to work without power. By hook or by crook, the images emerge from the developer fluid, recording the story of a city under siege.

In Boston, it is the worst blizzard in recorded history. 54 dead. 10,000 homeless and evacuated. There is no way to prepare for a storm that happens once every 200 years.

For their extraordinary effort in going out and getting the story, for the record they make of nature gone mad and human courage in the face of it, the Pulitzer Prize is awarded to the entire photographic staff of the *Boston Herald American*.

1980 The "Cleansing" of Iran

It is a wild, defiant land shaped by dense mountain chains and rivers that roar through craggy gorges. The people are equally wild and defiant, the land and its history riding in their hearts and reflected in their faces. That toughness and independence has been seared into their flesh by the burning 110° summer sun, then hardened by the lashing cold of their high-altitude winters. Just living the Kurdish life is a kind of curing process that has strengthened their resolve.

The Kurds are a warrior people, persisting in their fight for a national homeland. Their bodies are strapped with ammunition—strips of bullets lacing past bulbous grenades, which hang loosely from waist clips. Rifles are slung over shoulders or dangled off one hip or the other, though the historic dagger of the Kurdish martial past may also be secretly tucked away. Again and again, they have waged their military campaigns against a string of empires and countries who claimed to own them. The fight has become their crusade.

Tribes of them have combed this land for 4,000 years, yet sovereignty has eluded them. Surrounded by Turks, Syrians, Soviet Armenians, Iraqis, and Iranians, they have always been incorporated into one country or the other. They are like a nation of orphans. But in their hearts, they have carried their dream for Kurdish self-rule through centuries of homelessness, enriched by their own Kurd culture which is not Arabic, not Persian, not Turk.

In the past couple of decades, many Kurds have moved down from the mountains to establish themselves in Teheran, Baghdad, and other modern cities. City Kurds substitute fierce commitment to social justice for ancestral tribal loyalties. Many seem completely assimilated into urban life—as doctors, civil servants, journalists. Although there may be no outward trace of their tribal nomadic past, the city Kurd is strongly rooted to his people. During the 1970s' uprisings in Iraq, many city Kurds demonstrated those ties by abandoning their modern houses, cars, and TV sets to stand shoulder to shoulder with their kinsmen fighting in the hills.

The Kurd conflict in Iran is provoked by the Ayatollah Khomeini's Islamic Revolution in February of 1979. Seen as "God's personal agent on earth," his is a revolution of purification, one that promises to cleanse the soul of a nation debased by "satanic" Western influence. He establishes a fervent theocracy in the new Iran, galvanizing the country into strict alignment with the codes of the Shiia Islam sect.

The four million Kurds of Iran, followers of the Sunni sect of Islam, watch keenly the developments from the new government in Teheran and its vigorous promotion of the other main branch of Islam, the Shiia. Shiites feel that true Islam can only be revealed through the leadership of a line of divinely chosen imams, who are endowed exclusively with the "light" and wisdom to provide true guidance. However, Sunnis base their beliefs on the study of the Koran and its interpretations and the collected sayings of Mohammad. They do not uphold the notion of divine grace in their rulers.

The Kurds, a minority standing outside the new Shiia Islamic government, are suspicious and bitter. They have seen Kurdistan province overrun by Khomeini's Revolutionary Guard since the ouster of the Shah's regime, taking control of their courts, police, education . . . and lives. When in early spring, the government attempts to transfer the Kurds' wheat supply, as well as much of their bread, from Kurdistan to Teheran, the tension over autonomy explodes. In Sanandaj, their provincial capital, Kurd guerrillas face off against the army in savage street fighting. Moving from house to house, firing from alleyways and rooftops, the rebels try to run the army out of their capital. They temporarily seize the army garrison and some government buildings, but a week later, the army moves in convoys of tanks and helicopter gunships to crush the uprising.

In the Kurdish mind, the Islamic Republic is fast becoming just another dictatorship shrouded in ideology. As the months pass, the blood runs thick through Kurdistan. In a Middle Ages-style inquisition of butchery and beheadings, Khomeini's henchman, Ayatollah Khalkhali, travels from town to town conducting scores of executions. On August 27, a UPI photographer catches just one instance of "justice and cleansing" in the new Islamic Republic . . . the firing squad. Nine Kurd rebels and two former police officers of the deposed Shah are executed in Sanandaj, joining hundreds of others killed for "waging war on God and his representatives."

Still anonymous, the photographer's identity is withheld by UPI. If named, his life would be at risk.

1980 Feature
The Cowboy . . .
An American Folk Hero

Roundup . . . the cowboy's link through the decades and centuries, clear back to the Mexican vaqueros, to the thousands before them who have stiff-galloped a herd across open range and flanked and lassoed a calf for branding.

They suddenly break into view, rising above the small hill on the horizon. Ten men on horseback riding side by side through the stubbly, low-growing brush, kicking up a cloud of dust around them. One rider drops out of formation, moving back against the fence along the road. Riders continue to veer off, one by one, every few hundred yards as each of the ten, in turn, takes his position. Stretched out for half a mile, they advance into the pasture of calves and mother cows, prodding the herd along the fenceline. The cattle are packed tightly, one massive river of motion, rolling from one pasture to another on down the line. Every now and then, a cow breaks loose, and a cowboy rides it down.

All morning it will be drive, and then drive some more, until 300 head of cattle are pushed five miles to a holding pen, only the first step in the fall roundup.

The chow bell clangs at about 5:30 A.M., ringing out over the ranch long before first light. The bunkhouse stirs to life as the cowhands roll out of bed, into their duds, and over to the cookhouse. The married cowboys who live in single-family houses on the ranch follow the same schedule. Morning wash-ups pared down to a minimum, they gather at the cookhouse kitchen ten minutes later looking casual and unhurried.

The ranch hands lounge about the cookhouse, seated on kitchen counters, propped against walls, downing morning cups of coffee as they wait for final chow call. When it comes, and nobody has to be called twice, each grabs a seat on the benches that line the long table, often set for twenty-five or more. Large bowls heaped with scrambled eggs, hash browns, hot biscuits and gravy, bacon, pancakes and syrup make the rounds. Conversation trails off immediately. Within the space of ten minutes, the cookhouse is empty again . . . except for the cook, his wife, the man who keeps the ranch's windmills in tune, and a couple of repairmen called in to fix a water pump.

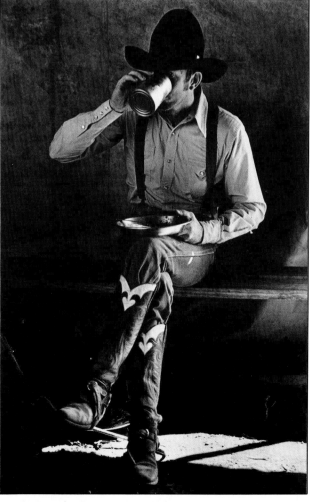

Out on the flat, open land of the Texas Panhandle's King County—population 600—Skeeter Hagler, of the *Dallas Times Herald* photographs roundup time on the neighboring Pitchfork and 6666 ranches. The two properties together total 370,000 acres. Legend has it that the Sixes Ranch got its name when the entire spread was won at a poker game with a hand of "6666."

There is a new breed of cowboy today, a skillful rider who handles not only horses, but helicopters. Foremost a cowboy, he knows cows—how, when, and why they move—and what they're up to. Called in as a spotter of stragglers, the pilot-cowboy coordinates with the ground crew by directing strays back to the herd.

Hagler: "The pilot was going to go up and shoo some cattle and asked me if I wanted to go along. We got up there and I found out he just doesn't fly normal. He started doing all this crazy stuff to get the cows moving—loops and dives. What he has to do is dive at them and pull up at the last minute to scare 'em. On the helicopter, he's got police sirens. He's got a red flag in his hand. He leans out the window, hollering, screaming, and waving the flag while he's got the sirens going. The guy flies using only one hand on the controls. It's really a sight. I was sicker 'n a sonovabitch afterwards—the other cowboys got a kick out of it, but since they're land types too, they related. I had passed the test."

Nothing reflects the legacy of cowboy pride quite like roping. It is their unfinished symphony. Casting a proper loop over a calf's hind legs, or heeling, is the foundation of the branding process. It is also essential to working the broncs and wild cattle. Maintaining that fine edge on their roping skill, they push to shave seconds and milliseconds from their times. Here are guys who rope the whole day long, especially during branding, who after they get done roping, go out and rope some more for fun.

Lunch either comes to you out on the range, chuck-wagon style, or you come to it, ranch cookhouse style. Most days, the cowboys just head back to the ranch and pile into the kitchen to wash up. The dirt, dried blood, horse sweat, and cow slobber from the morning's work has left its mark. After wolfing down their lunch, they file out the cookhouse door, one by one. This is their time for dallying. They might lay out under a shady tree or lean up against a post on the porch or stretch out on the bed of a pickup truck. Or they might round up a good ole cowboy bull session.

"These guys start telling stories about twenty years ago when a horse ran off with them and dragged them. What happens is, the story gets pretty dramatic, ya know. You look at some of the other cowboys and they're kinda rolling their eyes as if to say 'Oh, God, not this story again!' They've heard it a hundred times and it's always different. When you come across someone else later they say, 'Well, that stuff didn't really happen. What really happened is this . . .'"

Shooting the bull has been honed to high art. When a story gets told a hundred times to the same guys, it's got to get better each time. The extra punch assures an audience the next time the story is hauled out. The bull gets especially deep when there are city slickers around, like Dallas journalists. If you're a brand new audience, they make it real good for you.

"They talk a lot of horse. They talk about horses the way a mechanic talks about his tools. They're comparing 'em, talking about horses they've had, if this horse is better than that horse, on and on. They've all got this connection and if you're not in on it, you can get pretty lost."

A duststorm picked up during the afternoon, bringing on 35 mph winds and with it a good share of flying cockle burrs, stickers, and tumbleweed. This is the kind of weather when a cowboy's face disappears under a low-slung "ten gallon" and a high-tied bandanna, all except for a pair of eyes. Nobody enjoys an afternoon of chewing dirt.

The cowboy's day ends when he's through or when he gets to a stopping point. The young cowpuncher returns to his bunkhouse room—hot, sweaty, parched, and dirty from ten hours work on the open range. He forms a trough down the center of the white paper before filling it from end to end with Bugler's, lick-seals the edges, and rolls up a smoke. He lights up in the shadows of the wood-planked room, a lodging he will use for a month, or a season, before moving on. Except for his horse gear, his whole world lies before him in this room—a radio, a couple of sheets, a blanket, some shirts, some jeans, tobacco. This is a life of pick up and go when you want, and sit down and plant when you're ready. Cowboys call this freedom. Others might call it loneliness.

Oklahoma Territory . . . southwest of Mangum near the Texas/
Oklahoma border . . . 1916.

"It was a cold February day. My father was working on the
farm's windmill and watched silently as I saddled up my horse.
Neither one of us said anything. We just looked at one
another. I was eighteen and my parents weren't agreeable
about what I wanted to do. My dad and I didn't speak for
years . . ."

Young Tom Blasingame was running off to a life of horses
and cowboying, moving restlessly across the endless tract of
the Southwest. Brown, prickly, spare . . . a place without a
welcome mat. But in his time, he made a place for himself. He
saw his share of outlaw hideouts, train holdups, and frontier
socials. Mostly though, it was a harsh life of running cows and
learning horses, and vice versa, picking up everything he
needed to know along the way.

"There were dinners and dances at the camps almost
every weekend in the winter. You'd go twenty miles or more to
someone's house and there'd be lots of pretty girls. You
pushed back the furniture and danced in sets. I loved a good
waltz. Sometimes we'd ride broncos and show off for the girls.
The pies and cakes weren't hard to take either."

Tom Blasingame's land spreads out before him—the
Campbell Creek line camp on the JA Ranch. He lives here, by
himself, among the encroaching mesquite, in a weather-
bleached frame cabin near a creek lined with cottonwoods.
For the past twenty years, the old cowboy has worked this
country, riding its territory checking for downed fence or
windmills, water and range conditions, and stray cattle. At
eighty-one, he's still on the job, the oldest working cowboy in
America. He knows every rock and every prairie dog hole;

they've all been sized up on thousands of daily rounds just like
this one. He rides alone, crossing the 20,000 acre parcel of
the JA Ranch under his caretaking.

Snooks Sparks, JA wagon boss: "I'd rather have Tom
than three or four young cowboys. He's the same now as he
was when I met him in 1935. He's the perfect cowboy. He can
ride through a herd, ride out and tell you what's in there and
which calf belongs to which cow even when they're not
together. You just call out the horse you want in the corral,
and he gets him. He can recognize horses by their ears. He
can take the meanest bronc and gentle him in no time . . . And
he can still drive more cattle by himself than anyone I've ever
seen. He's got a way with them."

Getting to know these cowboys, Skeeter Hagler finds out
you don't get accepted too easily; you have to prove yourself.
You have to put your time in. Tom Beeler, cowboy-artist, said
it best: "They're dedicated. They're not in it for the money. It's
a pride, a way of life. They're doing the job and living up to it,
kind of a code almost. There's a code of the cowboy way of
life. You know, being a good horseman, knowing your
business and going about your business quietly and not
boasting, being honest and direct with people."

1981 Coup d'Etat

The symbols are familiar: the starred and striped design of the red, white, and blue flag; Capitol Hill with its domed Capitol building holding House and Senate chambers; the sound of English, spoken by soldiers named George Washington in towns called Virginia. Liberia was created in the image of America . . . Yankee-style democracy superimposed on nineteenth-century Africa.

The United States of 1820 was a white man's democracy; Liberia would be a black man's . . . developed as a free black settlement populated by freed slaves. Sponsored by the blue-blooded American Colonization Society, over the years 6,000 former slaves chose to sail to Africa . . . back to ancestry's call and freedom's promise. They carried with them in their ships the dream of liberty which had been held from them at arm's length. Liberia would be the chance for its fulfillment.

The original black settlers suffered from rampant malaria, TB, and sleeping sickness, but survived under the fraternal watch of Christian missionaries and the American Colonization Society. The fledgling community—called Monrovia—learned fast, expanding its territory in much the same way the United States did . . . land grabs accomplished through the trading of trinkets, weapons, and drink, and the signing of misleading treaties with native tribal chiefs. Tribal residents were pressed into service as field hands and domestics.

Threatened by the encroaching sweep of Liberia's reach, enraged tribes and competing European colonial powers challenged the settlers, but backed down under the threat of U.S. muscle. For the next generation, ACS-appointed white governors exercised a strong influence over their "creation." American presence was eventually subdued when Monrovia elected its own legislative council and went on a decade later, in 1847, to declare itself a free and independent republic.

While African nations have come and gone, there has always been Liberia, steadfast and strong. Maintaining the thread of stability through the chaos of post-World War II Africa, Liberia holds the fascination of American investment interests. Firestone Tire and Rubber Company had moved in early, establishing a rubber plantation on a million acres of tropics, at six cents an acre for ninety-nine years. In the process, it became a kingdom unto itself, a company town with its own police force, its own schools, its own jails, but no unions.

With the open-door policy of slave-descendent President William Tubman beginning in 1944, America was encouraged through generous business incentives to develop Liberia's resources. The invitation was enthusiastically accepted, ushering in an era of unparalleled economic growth . . . for some.

They travel in Mercedes limousines through downtown Monrovia, its steamy crowded streets lined with stalls where peddlers trade in safety pins, shoelaces, cigarettes, and whatever other odd items they can find; past intermittent patches of crumbling buildings; past the grimy port area; and on out to that part of town where an elite class lives well beyond the sight of poverty. Like plantation owners in blackface, these Americo-Liberian settler families have long fashioned for themselves an aristocracy of power and influence; the former slaves have become the masters.

The other 96 percent of the population, which call themselves "country people," make do with the same meager lot that they have always known. These are the indigenous Liberians, the descendents of the sixteen native tribes. For years, they have been forced nonparticipants in politics, education, and the mainstream economy. Many of them live in the steamy rain forests of the hinterlands in mud-walled huts where villages maintain themselves through subsistence agriculture. The restless ones find their way to Monrovia but almost certainly end up shantied at the edge of town in tents or under corrugated iron sheeting. They have been subjugated by their slave-lineaged countrymen who themselves came here to escape oppression. The equality so nobly cherished in the constitution has lost something in the translation.

Rising from the ranks of the indigenous population, Samuel Doe takes one of the few allotted steps on the status ladder allowable for a tribal descendent. He enlists in the army as a low-level noncom. This "advanced" position entitles Doe, along with his wife and four children, to a toolshed-sized hut—no plumbing, no doors or glassed-in windows, no flooring. All within sight of the sprawling executive mansion and the neighboring walled-in estates of the ruling black colonials. Like other soldiers, he is also granted tacit government approval to scavenge the countryside for food and other basics unobtainable on an enlisted man's paltry pay.

It is 2 A.M. In the darkness of April 12, 1980, Master Sergeant Doe, twenty-eight years old, and fifteen other ragtag enlistees in the Liberian army slip onto the grounds of the President's mansion. They move furtively across the expansive lawn, surprising the mansion guards stationed around the premises as they close in on the building. Cutting down guards along the way, they break inside. The assault group storms the corridors charging toward President William Tolbert's opulent living quarters. The soldiers, boiling with the anger of their people, gun him down and disembowel him amid the settees of the lavish antique decor. The rank and file rise in support of the takeover and empty the stockade of political prisoners.

Fort Worth Star-Telegram photographer Larry Price is sent to Liberia to document the condition of the Baptist missionaries there, many of whom had ties to Fort Worth through the Southwestern Baptist Theological Seminary. The whole country is incommunicado, still in the spasms of the coup. All night, Price can hear random gunshots in the street. A handwritten sign in the lobby of his hotel warns that anyone found on the streets after 6 P.M. curfew will be shot.

On April 22, having already visited the missionary schools and clinics, Price decides to cover the new head of state's fateful first press conference. Sergeant Doe speaks briefly, and then the minister of information comes in the back way and makes a casual announcement. "There will be some executions now down at the beach. Any of you who want to go had better hurry." In the space of a moment, an exotic but very manageable assignment turns bizarre.

More than 100°, drenched in humidity and emotional frenzy, the white beach seethes with thousands of ecstatic people. Those that can't attend can watch a live televised version. Posts are being driven into the sand. Price, the only American photographer present, breaks away from the small cluster of newspeople and, alone, walks toward the grotesque scene. He pushes close to the action, among pistol-waving soldiers, to take his photos. "I got right behind the soldiers who were lined up to do the shooting."

Thirteen of Tolbert's cabinet ministers have been led on a death march through the downtown streets, on their way to the beach site where they are to be executed for crimes of "high treason, rampant corruption, and gross violations of human rights." The posts stand mounted and secured. Nine of them, some wearing only rags wrapped around their waists, are led to the awaiting nine posts and roped in place. The revelry dies down as the soldiers take their place with upraised rifles in a now silent pause. "The ministers looked old and tired. They never said a word." The fire order brings a volley of blasts. And then the roaring of the rejoicing crowd.

Price: "The soldiers kept firing and other soldiers from all around ran up and fired at point-blank range with automatic rifles, with handguns, with almost every sort of gun. Several soldiers were reprimanded when they refused to stop firing." The remaining four are pushed forward and strapped in above the slumped bodies at their feet. "I got too close and with the crack of the final shots, a shell casing from one of the guns hit me above the eye."

Wild in celebration, the people mob the beach, dancing around the execution stakes. Like their white counterparts in Rhodesia, the colonialists of Liberia have fallen; the people have had their way. Out of this savage act comes hope for a new order. But is this a revolution, or just another African coup, to be followed by a new repressive power elite?

1981 **Feature**
Killing Time

For ten days in October of 1980, photographer Taro Yamasaki of the *Detroit Free Press* roams at will inside the State Prison of Southern Michigan at Jackson, the largest walled prison in the world. He is given this unprecedented freedom because in November, Michigan voters are going to be asked to approve a ballot proposal to increase prison funding. Prison officials are receptive to the feature story, wanting to demonstrate the dangerous overcrowding that exists at Jackson. But what Taro finds when the steel door clangs shut behind him goes far beyond the fact that 5,700 convicted felons are jammed together in a prison built to hold 4,000. He finds another world.

Fear and explosive tension saturate the atmosphere in the prison; the air presses down and lays on the skin like a filthy wet blanket. The blue-green institution-colored walls make the whole prison feel submerged, as if in an ocean of fear.

Among the inmates who cruise the halls and the yard are the predators and the prey. The prey are easily recognized. New inmates, called "fish," try to maintain their cool but they are scared, their movements unsure. Like wounded fish in the ocean, they appear different from those around them and are the first to be attacked.

Jack Brookes has spent fourteen of his thirty-one years in prison: "There's so much tension in here, you can never relax. You learn to always watch your back. You never know when someone will come at you. You can't trust anyone, even your friends. If you want to survive in here, you have to constantly prove that you're tougher, meaner, than the other guy. But even that'll only keep most of them from pressing you [for sex, money, or drugs]. You never know when the bug is going to go out on the guy standing next to you. I saw a man get cut from ear to ear because he wouldn't give up his breakfast roll. Can you imagine that . . . over a stale state breakfast roll?"

Yamasaki: "On a man's first day in the maximum-security area of Jackson Prison, he enters a cell like this and sees a bed, a toilet, a sink. That's it. For the next few years, or for life, this is his home. The most popular way of decorating one's cell is to display centerfolds from *Hustler* magazine. Some men cover the walls with family photos: of wife, children, parents. Some men have nothing but empty walls.

"There is very little real effort to keep drugs out of the prison. Any street drug from grass to heroin is easily available. A gallon of spud juice [homemade prison alcohol] costs ten dollars. Many of the officers think of drugs as a means of management. If the inmates are stoned, they are less likely to cause trouble."

Rehabilitation hasn't worked in most cases. The rate of recidivism is very high; many of the inmates who are paroled end up back here in a year. Most of the people in Jackson realize that what they did was wrong and that they never want to go back. But it would take an extraordinary person to live through the prison experience and be totally straight when he got out. Most of the inmates at Jackson are from the inner city of places like Detroit and Pontiac. The reality of their lives on the outside is that they are poor and uneducated. They talk about getting out with high hopes of living a straight life. But when they finally get out, they realize that they can't get work. It is hard enough to get a job; with a prison record, it's nearly impossible. So they end up robbing a gas station or a liquor store, or running some kind of scam. They want the good things in life, like anyone else.

The prison officials know they aren't rehabilitating; in fact, there is almost no control over the prisoner's actions. Because of the lack of funding, the prison is totally understaffed. What they settle for is to keep the inmates inside the walls. That's the bottom line. Many prisoners say that if it doesn't do anything else, prison makes you a better crook—smarter, tougher, more violent.

How easy is it to get weapons in the Big House?

Jack Brookes (not pictured): "A gun is expensive, five hundred dollars including ammunition. Shanks [knives] are easy. They're all made here—five dollars for a six-inch blade, four-inch handle, ten dollars for a ten-inch blade, four-inch handle; and for twenty dollars you can get a custom-made fourteen-inch blade. You can get it Bowie or dagger style, sharp on one side or both, and you can get it within two days of when you place your order."

During the summer between fifty and 100 knives are made in prison industries every day. In 1980, seventy-eight stabbings were reported. But prisoners only report a fraction of the knifings that take place. Naming the attacker makes you a snitch. Snitches are killed.

"In here, man, not having a knife ready is a death sentence."

146

Danny Aliff, on the left, a convicted sex offender: "When they break my door open in the morning, I walk out on that rock without any idea if I'll still be alive that night. It's rough when you're living in the jungle. There's just one law in here. Only the strong survive.

"Jackson's the end of the road. You ain't going to leave here the way you came in. You're going to leave bitter, angry, full of hate. Something's going to happen when you hit the street."

Yamasaki: "Cell Block 7 is called protective segregation. It is for inmates who are snitches, and for inmates who feel they could not protect themselves in the general population from being beaten, robbed, raped, or killed. There are inmates in Block 7 who have a price on their heads by other prisoners. Young white guys who are slight in build or handsome are often sent here because they would be constantly hit upon for sex in the yard.

"Of all the cell blocks, 7 is the most oppressive, the most eerie. The inmates are withdrawn and quiet—watching TV with blank expressions, or staring at the floor. They are prisoners among the prisoners, locked away from society and locked away from the prison itself. They are truly lost."

Block 5 is called the "hole." If you get a lot of tickets (minor infractions of the rules), you go into the hole. If you attack a guard, you go into the hole. If you are attacked or knifed and you refuse to snitch, you go into the hole. The hole is the worst place to be. You are isolated from all the other people in the world. Some prisoners go crazy in the hole.

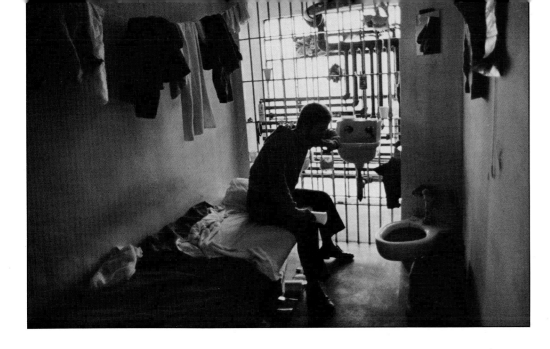

The November ballot proposal to increase prison funding is defeated. Five months later, Jackson explodes. After an attack on two guards by inmates wielding sharpened broom handles, guards, frustrated over the dangerous understaffing, attempt a massive weapons shakedown and a general lockdown. More than 1,200 maximum-security inmates rise up, seizing two cell blocks and breaking out of two others, looting and setting fires to the hated prison. Locked away from society's averted eyes, the festering problem of inhuman prisons continues to create living time bombs.

1982 Six Bullets

For AP photographer Ron Edmonds, this is all very routine. He is standing on the street side of the president's limousine, waiting in a warm springtime drizzle for President Reagan to emerge from the Washington Hilton Hotel. A member of the presidential travel pool, his job is to be there when the President of the United States is on the move. He is there when the president arrives and he is there when the president departs.

The police have the crowd cordoned off across the street behind him. He takes a standard position, shooting across the roof of the limo, to get a shot of the president waving, or maybe a child running out of the crowd and getting a kiss. It makes for a nice picture.

Once he has a few photos of the president coming out, he will wait for him to get into the limousine and then, as usual, he will have to race back to the press van, six or seven cars back in the motorcade, in time to take off. Edmonds checks his equipment, getting ready for the shot.

At this moment, President Reagan is walking casually through a secured passageway from the stage, where he had spoken, toward the street. He is at ease, chatting with his aides Press Secretary James Brady and Deputy Chief of Staff Michael Deaver. It had been a routine speech on his economic program, to 3,500 AFL-CIO delegates. This is his seventieth day in office, and things are running smoothly. At 2:25 in the afternoon, they open the two steel doors of the private VIP entrance, and he walks into the mist and the cheers.

Waiting for him in the crowd is John W. Hinckley. This is not a routine day for him. This is the biggest moment of his life. After years of meaningless drifting, he has been delivered into the political heart of the nation by a Greyhound bus from nowhere in particular.

A loner, Hinckley's world is a mix of Nazis, movie stars, guns, and fast-food hamburgers. His life had been a cipher until 1978, when he tried to join the Nazi party . . . he was thrown out for being too violent and too crazy. Later, he was arrested in Nashville for trying to carry guns onto a plane. It was the same day President Carter was in town. Yet, his name is not on any list of people who could be dangerous to the president. An hour ago, in his hotel room, he wrote a letter to the actress Jodie Foster, made famous by her role as a child prostitute in the film *Taxi Driver,* Hinckley's blueprint for fame. He has hovered around her for months.

"Dear Jodie:
There is a definite possibility that I will be killed in my attempt to get Reagan. It is for this very reason that I am writing you this letter now . . .
[It ends] Jodie, I'm asking you to please look into your heart and at least give me the chance with this historical deed to gain your respect and love.
I love you forever. John Hinckley"

Twenty-five years old, from an oil-rich, conservative family, he is the dark flip side of the American Dream . . . but no one ever heard him ticking. His usual blank stare has been replaced by an agitated impatience. He clutches the pistol in his sweaty hand. He is about to become Somebody.

President Reagan walks toward the limousine, smiling and waving to the crowd across the driveway. Then, a reporter in the press section to his left tries to plug in a quick question. "Mr. President, Mr. President?" Reagan, now only three feet from the car, lifts his arm in recognition.

John Hinckley, who has somehow made his way into the press section, reaches his hand out of his raincoat. He holds a snub-nosed .22 caliber "Saturday night special," the cylinder loaded with six Devastator bullets, which are designed to explode on impact. Crouching, with both hands steadying the pistol, he opens fire.

For an instant, Reagan sees the gunman firing at him and he seems to freeze in shock. He is looking at death, and he himself is helpless to stop it.

John Hinckley fires all six shots in 1.9 seconds. One of the first bullets slams into James Brady's forehead above his left eye, exploding inside his brain. He pitches forward, blood pouring out of his head into an iron grate in the sidewalk.

Michael Deaver, also in the line of fire, ducks and lunges for cover behind the limousine. So close is he to the shots that he feels the concussion of the bullets and smells the powder from the gun. A bullet whines by his shoulder, just missing Ron

Edmonds' head, and hits a window across the street.

Washington, D.C., policeman Thomas Delahanty, standing in front of Hinckley, spins and falls to the cement, a bullet in his neck. Screaming in pain, he struggles to rise but cannot.

There are three Devastator bullets left . . . but the Secret Service men at the president's side are reacting even faster than Hinckley can fire. Agent Timothy McCarthy (who can be seen to the far right in the three-frame sequence) whirls at the sound of gunfire and places his body in front of the president as a shield. He is instantly hit in the chest. (In the third photograph of the sequence, the bullet has just smashed into his chest, and he is beginning to react.) The bullet lifts him up and spinning sideways, he drops to the pavement.

At the first shot, Agent Jerry Parr, standing behind President Reagan, hurls the stunned president through the open door onto the floor of the limo. As he does, another bullet smacks into the window of the open door just as the president is moving past it. But the bulletproof glass stops it cold.

The aim of the final bullet is off, hitting the side of the limousine. But careening off the car, the bullet moves through the space made by the open door. In the millisecond that the president is hurtling through that space, the trajectory of the bullet finds him. By now the size of a dime, the bullet slices into his side under his left armpit, glances off a rib, and punctures his lung, stopping near his heart.

"Take off!" Agent Parr screams at the driver as he and the president land on the floor. "Just take off!" and the black Lincoln roars out of the driveway.

Ron Edmonds had just started to take the picture when the first pop went off. "I saw his grimace through the viewfinder as I squeezed the shutter down. To give you an idea of how fast the whole thing happened, I was shooting with a motor drive, which shoots about five frames a second. I have five frames in a row of this scene, of which only three have President Reagan in the picture. In the last two frames, he has already been pushed out of sight beneath the limousine top.

"When I heard the pops, my first reaction was that firecrackers had gone off. During the campaign, that had happened a number of times. The people who went down were out of my viewfinder to the right. I didn't even know they were hit until the limo pulled away."

Edmonds turns to the right as the car speeds off, seeing for the first time the carnage. Three bodies lie sprawled on the pavement. The acrid smell of gunpowder lingers in the damp air.

Standing in the midst of the chaos, another Secret Service agent readies his Uzi submachine gun in case of a further

attack and, ironically, to protect the life of the would-be assassin. John Hinckley struggles violently with police and agents but is finally handcuffed and hurried away.

Edmonds: "The Secret Service did a remarkable job. It was like a textbook training film but in real life. Their instinctive reaction and great personal courage, as well as the bullets taken by Jim Brady, Officer Delahanty, and Agent McCarthy, probably saved the president's life."

As they pull away from the curb, neither Agent Parr nor the president himself know that he is hit. "It felt like a hammer hit me," the president later said. But he assumes the pain is from being thrown into the car. Suddenly, he begins to cough up blood. They race to the hospital, and once again a nation holds its breath, wondering if they have lost a president.

Edmonds: "The political system in America demands that presidents get out there and press the flesh. There is no way to totally protect him, it is impossible. Anyone willing to trade his life for the president's can do it. The Secret Service can only cut down the odds. In this case, they almost totally shielded him; he was only exposed for an instant. But that's all it took."

We have gotten to be old hands at this terrible drama . . . the initial shock and anger, the sad vigil by the television set with the endless slow motion replays, and the numbed acceptance. The blank-faced assassins continue to act out their

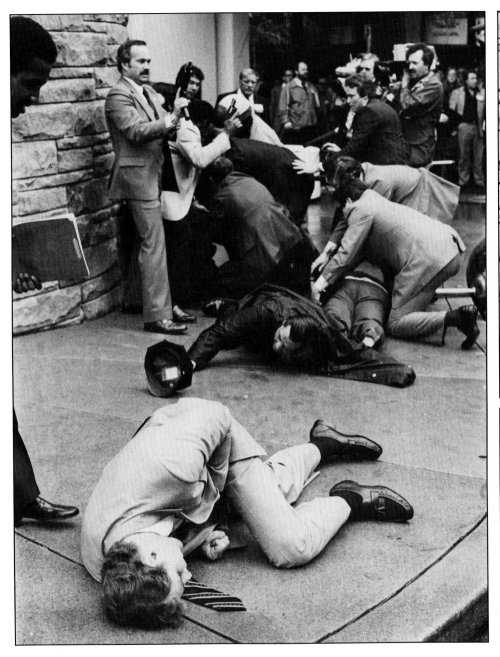

fantasies in such an easy way. For John Hinckley, getting a cheap "Saturday night special" was not much more difficult than getting a hamburger to go.

John Hinckley is found not guilty by reason of insanity. He is now in a mental institution.

Reference Information

YEAR: 1942
PHOTOGRAPHER: Milton (Pete) Brooks
COPYRIGHT: Wide World Photos
*AFFILIATION: *Detroit News*
DATE: April 2, 1941

EQUIPMENT: 4 x 5 Speed Graphic
Kodak film
NOTES: First award

YEAR: 1943
PHOTOGRAPHER: Frank (Pappy) Noel
COPYRIGHT: Wide World Photos
AFFILIATION: Associated Press
DATE: January, 1942

EQUIPMENT: 4 x 5 Speed Graphic
Kodak film

YEAR: 1944
PHOTOGRAPHER: Frank Filan
COPYRIGHT: Wide World Photos
AFFILIATION: Associated Press
DATE: November 22, 1943

EQUIPMENT: 4 x 5 Speed Graphic
Kodak film
NOTES: In this year, there are two winners. This is the award for wartime photography.

YEAR: 1944
PHOTOGRAPHER: Earl Bunker
COPYRIGHT: Wide World Photos
AFFILIATION: *Omaha World-Herald*
DATE: July 15, 1943

EQUIPMENT: 4 x 5 Speed Graphic
Kodak film
NOTES: In this year, there are two winners. This is the award for peacetime photography.

*All affiliations are at the time of award.

YEAR: 1945
PHOTOGRAPHER: Joe Rosenthal
COPYRIGHT: Wide World Photos
AFFILIATION: Associated Press
DATE: February 23, 1945

EQUIPMENT: 4 x 5 Speed Graphic
Between f/8 and f/11,
1/400 second
Agfa film
NOTES: As a rule, all Pulitzer Prize photographs are awarded for work done in the previous year. An exception is made in the case of this classic photograph.

YEAR: 1946
No award

YEAR: 1947
PHOTOGRAPHER: Arnold Hardy
COPYRIGHT: Wide World Photos
DATE: December 7, 1946

EQUIPMENT: 4 x 5 Speed Graphic
Kodak film
NOTES: First amateur

YEAR: 1948
PHOTOGRAPHER: Frank Cushing
COPYRIGHT: Wide World Photos
AFFILIATION: *Boston Traveler*
DATE: June 23, 1947

EQUIPMENT: 4 x 5 Speed Graphic
Kodak film

YEAR: 1949
PHOTOGRAPHER: Nathaniel Fein
COPYRIGHT: Wide World Photos
AFFILIATION: *New York Herald-Tribune*
DATE: June 14, 1948

EQUIPMENT: 4 x 5 Speed Graphic
f/5.6, 1/100 second
Agfa film (200 ASA)

YEAR	1950
PHOTOGRAPHER	Bill Crouch
COPYRIGHT	Wide World Photos
AFFILIATION	*Oakland Tribune*
DATE	October 2, 1949
EQUIPMENT	4 x 5 Speed Graphic
	Kodak film

YEAR	1951
PHOTOGRAPHER	Max Desfor
COPYRIGHT	Wide World Photos
AFFILIATION	Associated Press
DATE	December 5, 1950
EQUIPMENT	4 x 5 Speed Graphic
	Kodak film
NOTES	A series, of which this photograph is representative

YEAR	1952
PHOTOGRAPHER	John Robinson/Don Ultang
COPYRIGHT	Wide World Photos
AFFILIATION	*Des Moines Register & Tribune*
DATE	October 20, 1951
EQUIPMENT	4 x 5 Speed Graphic with 20-inch lens
	Kodak Super Pan film
NOTES	(EYMO) Bell & Howell, 35-mm movie camera, Kodak film. A series. Robinson's movie camera recorded a sequence of the entire play. Ultang's single shot, the last photograph in the series, clearly records the illegal blow, plus the fact that Bright was obviously out of play. Thus, they shared the prize.

YEAR	1953
PHOTOGRAPHER	Bill Gallagher
COPYRIGHT	Wide World Photos
AFFILIATION	*Flint Journal*
DATE	September 2, 1952
EQUIPMENT	4 x 5 Speed Graphic
	Kodak film

YEAR	1954
PHOTOGRAPHER	Virginia Schau
COPYRIGHT	Wide World Photos
DATE	May 3, 1953
EQUIPMENT	Kodak Brownie
	Kodak film
NOTES	Amateur. First woman to win

YEAR	1955
PHOTOGRAPHER	Jack Gaunt
COPYRIGHT	Wide World Photos
AFFILIATION	*Los Angeles Times*
DATE	April 2, 1954
EQUIPMENT	Rolleiflex
	f/16, 1/250 second
	Kodak film

YEAR	1956
PHOTOGRAPHER	George Mattson
COPYRIGHT	Wide World Photos
AFFILIATION	*New York Daily News*
DATE	November 2, 1955
EQUIPMENT	Varied
NOTES	A series. The Pulitzer Prize was awarded to the entire photographic staff of the *Daily News* for their coverage of life in New York City in 1955, of which George Mattson's photograph is representative. The following photographers are represented: Al Amy, Paul Bernius, Ed Clarity, Jack Clarity, Tom Cunningham, Jack Eckert, Albert Fougel, Tom Gallagher, Ed Giorandino, Phil Greitzer, Charles Hoff, Frank Hurley, Walter Kelleher, Bob Koller, Hal Mathewson, George Mattson, Fred Morgan, Charles Payne, Ed Peters, Joe Petrella, Sam Platnick, Al Pucci, Gordon Rynders, Nick Sorrentino, Paul Thayer, and Seymour Wally.

YEAR	1957
PHOTOGRAPHER	Harry Trask
COPYRIGHT	Wide World Photos
AFFILIATION	*Boston Traveler*
DATE	July 26, 1956
EQUIPMENT	4 x 5 Speed Graphic
	f/5.6
	Kodak Royal Pan film (400 ASA)

YEAR	1958
PHOTOGRAPHER	Bill Beall
COPYRIGHT	Bill Beall
AFFILIATION	*Washington Daily News*
DATE	September 10, 1957
EQUIPMENT	4 x 5 Speed Graphic
	f/16 at 1/100 second
	Kodak Super Pan film

YEAR	1959
PHOTOGRAPHER	Bill Seaman
COPYRIGHT	Wide World Photos
AFFILIATION	*Minneapolis Star-Tribune*
DATE	May 16, 1958
EQUIPMENT	Rolleiflex
	Kodak Tri-X film

YEAR	1960
PHOTOGRAPHER	Andrew Lopez
COPYRIGHT	United Press International
AFFILIATION	United Press International
DATE	January 17, 1959
EQUIPMENT	Rolleiflex, 80-mm lens
	Kodak Tri-X film
NOTES	A series

YEAR	1961
PHOTOGRAPHER	Yasushi Nagao
COPYRIGHT	United Press International
AFFILIATION	*Mainichi Shimbun*
DATE	October 12, 1960
EQUIPMENT	4 x 5 Speed Graphic
NOTES	First foreign winner. He became eligible for the Pulitzer when his photograph was published in U.S. newspapers.

YEAR	1962
PHOTOGRAPHER	Paul Vathis
COPYRIGHT	Wide World Photos
AFFILIATION	Associated Press
DATE	April 22, 1961
EQUIPMENT	Hasselblad, 180-mm lens
	Kodak Tri-X film

YEAR	1963
PHOTOGRAPHER	Hector Rondon
COPYRIGHT	Hector Rondon
AFFILIATION	*La Republica*
DATE	June 4, 1962
EQUIPMENT	Leica
	Kodak Tri-X film

YEAR	1964
PHOTOGRAPHER	Robert Jackson
COPYRIGHT	Robert Jackson
AFFILIATION	*Dallas Times Herald*
DATE	November 24, 1963
EQUIPMENT	Nikon, 35-mm lens
	Kodak Tri-X film

YEAR	1965
PHOTOGRAPHER	Horst Faas
COPYRIGHT	Wide World Photos
AFFILIATION	Associated Press
DATE	1964
EQUIPMENT	Leica, 35-mm, 90-mm
	and 200-mm lenses
NOTES	A series

YEAR	1966
PHOTOGRAPHER	Kyoichi Sawada
COPYRIGHT	United Press International
AFFILIATION	United Press International
DATE	February-August, 1965
EQUIPMENT	Nikon
	Kodak Tri-X film
NOTES	A series

YEAR	1967
PHOTOGRAPHER	Jack Thornell
COPYRIGHT	Wide World Photos
AFFILIATION	Associated Press
DATE	June 6, 1966
EQUIPMENT	Nikon, 105-mm lens
	Kodak Tri-X film
NOTES	A series

YEAR	1968
PHOTOGRAPHER	Rocco Morabito
COPYRIGHT	Wide World Photos
AFFILIATION	*Jacksonville Journal*
DATE	July 17, 1967
EQUIPMENT	Rolleiflex
	f/8 at 1/500 second
	Kodak Tri-X film

YEAR	1968 Feature
PHOTOGRAPHER	Toshio Sakai
COPYRIGHT	United Press International
AFFILIATION	United Press International
DATE	June, 1967
EQUIPMENT	Nikon
NOTES	First feature photography award

YEAR	1969
PHOTOGRAPHER	Edward Adams
COPYRIGHT	Wide World Photos
AFFILIATION	Associated Press
DATE	February 1, 1968
EQUIPMENT	Nikon, 35-mm lens
	f/11 at 1/500 second
	Kodak Tri-X film

YEAR	1969 Feature
PHOTOGRAPHER	Moneta Sleet, Jr.
COPYRIGHT	*Ebony* magazine, Johnson Publishing Company
AFFILIATION	*Ebony* magazine
DATE	April 9, 1968
EQUIPMENT	Nikon, Kodak Tri-X film
NOTES	First black photographer to win. A magazine photographer, he became eligible when his photograph was published in U.S. newspapers.

YEAR	1970
PHOTOGRAPHER	Steve Starr
COPYRIGHT	Wide World Photos
AFFILIATION	Associated Press
DATE	April 20, 1969
EQUIPMENT	Nikon, 28-mm lens
	Kodak Tri-X film

YEAR	1970 Feature
PHOTOGRAPHER	Dallas Kinney
COPYRIGHT	Dallas Kinney
AFFILIATION	*Palm Beach Post*
DATE	1969
EQUIPMENT	Nikon and Leica, 20-mm, 35-mm, 85-mm, 200-mm lenses
	Kodak Tri-X film
NOTES	A series

YEAR	1971
PHOTOGRAPHER	John Filo
COPYRIGHT	*Valley News-Dispatch,* Tarentum, Pennsylvania
AFFILIATION	*Valley Daily News & Daily Dispatch*
DATE	May 4, 1970
EQUIPMENT	Nikormat, 43-mm–86-mm zoom lens
	Kodak Tri-X film
NOTES	Filo was a journalism student at Kent State University at the time.

YEAR	1971 Feature
PHOTOGRAPHER	Jack Dykinga
COPYRIGHT	*Chicago Sun-Times*
AFFILIATION	*Chicago Sun-Times*
DATE	July 26-29, 1970
EQUIPMENT	Nikon
	Kodak Tri-X film
NOTES	A series

YEAR	1972
PHOTOGRAPHER	Horst Faas/Michel Laurent
COPYRIGHT	Wide World Photos
AFFILIATION	Associated Press
DATE	December 18, 1971
EQUIPMENT	Leica, 35-mm, 90-mm and 200-mm lenses Kodak Tri-X film
NOTES	A series. Faas was the first photographer to win two Pulitzer Prizes

YEAR	1972 Feature
PHOTOGRAPHER	David Kennerly
COPYRIGHT	United Press International
AFFILIATION	United Press International
DATE	1971
EQUIPMENT	Nikon Kodak Tri-X film
NOTES	A series

YEAR	1973
PHOTOGRAPHER	Huynh Cong Ut
COPYRIGHT	Wide World Photos
AFFILIATION	Associated Press
DATE	June 8, 1972
EQUIPMENT	Leica Kodak Tri-X film

YEAR	1973 Feature
PHOTOGRAPHER	Brian Lanker
COPYRIGHT	Brian Lanker
AFFILIATION	Topeka Capital-Journal
DATE	January 27, 1972
EQUIPMENT	Nikon, 24-mm, 35-mm and 105-mm lenses Kodak Tri-X film
NOTES	A series

YEAR	1974
PHOTOGRAPHER	Anthony Roberts
COPYRIGHT	Wide World Photos
DATE	November 23, 1973
EQUIPMENT	Nikon Kodak Tri-X film
NOTES	A series. Free-lance photographer

YEAR	1974 Feature
PHOTOGRAPHER	Sal Veder
COPYRIGHT	Wide World Photos
AFFILIATION	Associated Press
DATE	March 17, 1973
EQUIPMENT	Nikon, 200-mm lens f/8 at 1/500 second Kodak Tri-X film

YEAR	1975
PHOTOGRAPHER	Gerald Gay
COPYRIGHT	Seattle Times
AFFILIATION	Seattle Times
DATE	October 11, 1974
EQUIPMENT	Nikon, 28-mm lens f/8 at 1/125 Kodak Tri-X film

YEAR	1975 Feature
PHOTOGRAPHER	Matthew Lewis
COPYRIGHT	Washington Post
AFFILIATION	Washington Post Sunday magazine supplement, Potomac
DATE	1974
EQUIPMENT	Nikon Kodak Ektachrome X film and Kodak Tri-X film
NOTES	A series. First award that included color photographs

YEAR	1976
PHOTOGRAPHER	Stanley J. Forman
COPYRIGHT	Boston Herald-American
AFFILIATION	Boston Herald-American
DATE	July 22, 1975
EQUIPMENT	Nikon, 35-mm and 135-mm lenses f/8 at 1/250 second Kodak Tri-X film
NOTES	A series

YEAR	1976 Feature
PHOTOGRAPHER	Entire photographic staff
COPYRIGHT	The Courier-Journal; The Louisville Times
AFFILIATION	The Courier-Journal; The Louisville Times

DATE	August–December, 1975
EQUIPMENT	Nikon and Leica
	Kodak Tri-X film
NOTES	A series. The 17 staff photographers: Cort Best, Michael Coers, Melissa Farlow, Stan Denny, C. Thomas Hardin, Tom R. Hayes, Bud Kamenish, Frank Kimmel, Charles William Luster, Bryan L. Moss, Richard Nugent, Paul Schuhmann, Pam Spaulding, Larry R. Spitzer, Robert Steinau, William Strode, and Keith Williams

YEAR	1977
PHOTOGRAPHER	Neal Ulevich
COPYRIGHT	Wide World Photos
AFFILIATION	Associated Press
DATE	October 6, 1976
EQUIPMENT	Nikon
	Kodak Tri-X film
NOTES	A series. One of the two spot news awards this year

YEAR	1977
PHOTOGRAPHER	Stanley J. Forman
COPYRIGHT	*Boston Herald-American*
AFFILIATION	*Boston Herald-American*
DATE	April 5, 1976
EQUIPMENT	Nikon, 20-mm lens
	Kodak Tri-X film
NOTES	First photographer to win two consecutive Pulitzer Prizes. One of the two spot news awards this year

YEAR	1977 Feature
PHOTOGRAPHER	Robin Hood
COPYRIGHT	Wide World Photos
AFFILIATION	*Chattanooga News-Free Press*
DATE	May 15, 1976
EQUIPMENT	Nikon, 105-mm lens
	Kodak Tri-X film

YEAR	1978
PHOTOGRAPHER	John Blair
COPYRIGHT	John Blair
AFFILIATION	Free-lance
DATE	February 10, 1977
EQUIPMENT	Pentax Spotmatic, 28-mm (3.5) Takumar lens
	f/5.6 at 1/60 second
	Kodak Tri-X film
NOTES	Initially awarded in error to UPI photographer Jim Schweiker, due to a misidentification of the photographer by UPI

YEAR	1978 Feature
PHOTOGRAPHER	J. Ross Baughman
COPYRIGHT	J. Ross Baughman
AFFILIATION	Associated Press
DATE	December 2, 1977
EQUIPMENT	Leica M-4, 35-mm Summicron lens (lineup and man with bat)
	f/8 at 1/500 second
	Leicaflex SL2, 24-mm Elmarit lens (man in noose)
	f/2.8 at 1/15 second
	Ilford HP4 film
NOTES	A series of 3

YEAR	1979
PHOTOGRAPHER	Thomas J. Kelly III
COPYRIGHT	Thomas J. Kelly III
AFFILIATION	*The Mercury* (Pottstown, Pa.)
DATE	May 10, 1978
EQUIPMENT	Fujica ST-701 (2), 28-mm Pentax Takumar lens,135-mm Vivitar lens
	f/5.6 to f/8 at 1/500 second
	Kodak Tri-X film
NOTES	First photographer to win from a small-town newspaper.
	A series of 13

YEAR	1979 Feature
PHOTOGRAPHER	Entire photographic staff
COPYRIGHT	*Boston Herald American*—Boston Newspaper Division of the Hearst Corporation
AFFILIATION	*Boston Herald American*
DATE	February 6, 7, and 8, 1978
EQUIPMENT	Nikon F, assorted lenses
NOTES	The 16 staff photographers: Kevin Cole, M. Leo Tierney, Paul Benoit, Gene Dixon, Mike Andersen, Bob Howard, Roland Oxton, Ray Lussier, Angela Kaloventzos, Ted Gartland, Dick Thomson, Frank Hill, Leo Renahan, Stanley Forman, Dennis Brearley, John Thompson. Third Pulitzer Prize award for Stanley Forman. A series of 20

YEAR	1980
PHOTOGRAPHER	Anonymous
COPYRIGHT	United Press International
AFFILIATION	United Press International
DATE	August 27, 1979
EQUIPMENT	Unknown
NOTES	First unnamed photographer

YEAR	1980 Feature
PHOTOGRAPHER	Skeeter Hagler
COPYRIGHT	Skeeter Hagler
AFFILIATION	*Dallas Times Herald*
DATE	9 days in October and November of 1979
EQUIPMENT	Nikon F, F2, and FE, 20-mm, 35-mm, 55-mm macro, 85-mm, 180-mm, 300-mm, and 600-mm lenses. Kodak Tri-X and Kodachrome
NOTES	A series of 20

YEAR	1981
PHOTOGRAPHER	Larry C. Price
COPYRIGHT	Larry C. Price and *Fort Worth Star-Telegram*
AFFILIATION	*Fort Worth Star-Telegram*
DATE	April 22, 1980
EQUIPMENT	Nikon FE, Leica Rangefinder, 20-mm, 35-mm, 105-mm and 300-mm lenses. f/16 at 1/250 second and f/8 at 1/60 second. Kodak Tri-X film
NOTES	A series of 10

YEAR	1981 Feature
PHOTOGRAPHER	Taro Yamasaki
COPYRIGHT	Taro Yamasaki and *Detroit Free Press*
AFFILIATION	*Detroit Free Press*
DATE	10 days in October and November of 1980
EQUIPMENT	Nikon F2, 24-mm, 35-mm, 85-mm, and 180-mm lenses. Kodacolor 400 and Kodak Tri-X
NOTES	A series of 50

YEAR	1982
PHOTOGRAPHER	Ron Edmonds
COPYRIGHT	Wide World Photos
AFFILIATION	Associated Press
DATE	March 30, 1981
EQUIPMENT	Nikon F3, 50-mm lens (3-picture car sequence), 85-mm lens (agent with Uzi), and 35-mm lens (wrestling assailant on ground). Kodak Tri-X film
NOTES	A series of 8